Major Sociocultural Trends Shaping the Contemporary World

Major Sociocultural Trends Shaping the Contemporary World

K.H. Yeganeh

BEP BUSINESS EXPERT PRESS

Major Sociocultural Trends Shaping the Contemporary World

First published in 2018 by
Business Expert Press, LLC
222 East 46th Street, New York, NY 10017
www.businessexpertpress.com

ISBN-13: 978-1-63157-787-1 (paperback)
ISBN-13: 978-1-63157-788-8 (e-book)

Business Expert Press International Business Collection

Collection ISSN: 1948-2752 (print)
Collection ISSN: 1948-2760 (electronic)

Cover and interior design by Exeter Premedia Services Private Ltd., Chennai, India

First edition: 2018

10 9 8 7 6 5 4 3 2 1

Printed in the United States of America.

Abstract

The current volume offers a concise and analytical portrait of the contemporary world. The author encompasses concepts and theories from multiple disciplines notably sociology, anthropology, international relations, and economics to examine the major sociocultural transformations of the modern world, their underlying causes, and their consequences. The volume is organized in 10 chapters dealing with a variety of topics including global demographic trends, globalization, culture, foreign affairs, emerging markets, environmental degradation, global security, global health, large corporations, and economic inequality. Each chapter is divided into separate sections examining the accompanying themes.

This book is a valuable reference for managers and business leaders, students, policy makers, and all those who are interested in acquiring a better understanding of the sociocultural trends that are shaping our world.

Keywords

culture, economic inequality, emerging markets, environmental degradation, foreign affairs, global demographics, global health, global security, globalization, large corporations, sociocultural trends, super-rich

Contents

CHAPTER 1

Global Demographic Trends

An Incredible Growth of Human Population

Throughout most of human history, for thousands of years, the world population growth has been very slow. For instance, it is estimated that the world's population grew slowly from about 2.4 million people in 10000 BCE to 295 million in 1000 CE [27]. Only 200 years ago there were less than 1 billion human beings living on earth. Since the 18th century with the advent of industrial revolution and advances in medicine, agriculture, and sanitation, the world population has increased exponentially. Around the 1830s, the world population reached 1 billion for the first time. It took another century for the world population to hit 2 billion around the 1930s. The third billion was reached only 30 years later in the 1960s. Since then, the world population has grown very rapidly soaring to a colossal number of 7 billion in 2011 (see Table 1.1 and Figure 1.1). In other words, the world population has witnessed an astonishing surge of 133 percent only in 50 years between 1960 and 2011. At the time of this writing (mid-2017), the world population is 7.6 billion and it is expected to rise another 100 million by the end of the year. Accordingly, the world's population has increased by approximately 1 billion

Table 1.1 World population historical data

Year	Population	Yearly change (%)	Yearly change	Urban population (%)	Urban population
2017	7,515,284,153	1.11	82,620,878	54.70	4,110,778,369
2016	7,432,663,275	1.13	83,191,176	54.30	4,034,193,153
2015	7,349,472,099	1.18	83,949,411	53.80	3,957,285,013
2010	6,929,725,043	1.23	82,017,839	51.50	3,571,272,167
2005	6,519,635,850	1.25	78,602,746	49.10	3,199,013,076
2000	6,126,622,121	1.33	78,299,807	46.60	2,856,131,072
1995	5,735,123,084	1.55	85,091,077	44.80	2,568,062,984
1990	5,309,667,699	1.82	91,425,426	43	2,285,030,904
1985	4,852,540,569	1.79	82,581,621	41.30	2,003,049,795
1980	4,439,632,465	1.80	75,646,647	39.40	1,749,539,272
1975	4,061,399,228	1.98	75,782,307	37.80	1,534,721,238
1970	3,682,487,691	2.08	71,998,514	36.70	1,350,280,789
1965	3,322,495,121	1.94	60,830,259	N.A.	N.A.
1960	3,018,343,828	1.82	52,005,861	33.80	1,019,494,911
1955	2,758,314,525	1.78	46,633,043	N.A.	N.A.

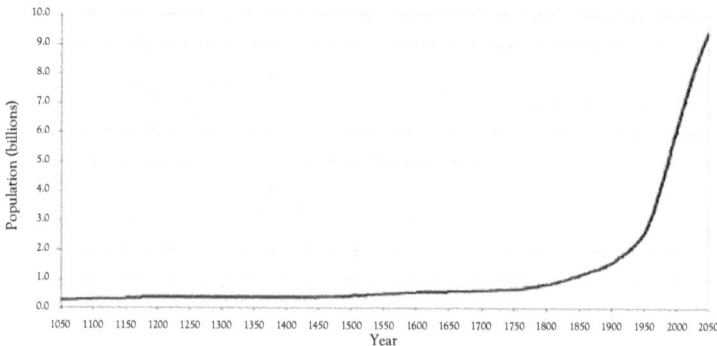

Figure 1.1 World population growth over time, 1050–2050

over the last 12 years. The surge in population growth rates in the 1950s and 1960s was caused mainly by quick declines in death rates across the developing world [1, 2, 3]. According to the United Nations Population Division, the world population is expected to exceed 8 billion in 2024,

9 billion in 2038, and 10 billion in 2056. If these predictions come true, the world population will see an increase of 7 billion in 100 years between 1956 and 2056 or an astonishing growth of almost 234 percent! To put it in perspective, 10 billion would be the equivalent of adding China and India's populations to the present world population [4]. Because of a very fast population growth between the 1950s and the 1970s, many countries encountered difficulty in implementing their development plans and introduced birth control and family planning programs. Subsequently, population growth rate fairly slowed down in the 1990s. Due to the birth control programs and contagious diseases such as AIDS/HIV, currently, the world population grows more slowly than in the 1970s and 1980s.

Historically, it is possible to identify three major phases in the world's population growth. The first phase was premodern era or the period before the 17th century when population growth was very slow due to a combination of factors including a shortage of food resources and lower levels of life expectancy. The second phase began in the 18th century with the arrival of modernity and was marked by rising standards of living and improving health. The third phase started in the 1980s and the population growth rate, particularly in developed countries, is falling [27]. Despite the slackening growth, the world population will continue to grow in short- and mid-term because the fertility rates in developing countries are still high and survival rates are poised to improve. Therefore, continued population growth until 2050 is almost certain. Based on recent assessments, the global population will be hovering between 8.4 and 8.6 billion in 2030 and between 9.5 and 13.3 billion in 2100 [5].

In addition to the global population growth, we should pay attention to the distribution, the density, and the uneven patterns of growth across the world as these issues imply important consequences. At the present, 4.5 billion people or an equivalent of 60 percent of the world's population live in Asia making it the most populous continent. After Asia, Africa hosts 1.3 billion people or 16 percent of the world's population, while Europe with a population of 742 million and Latin America and the Caribbean with 646 million respectively contain 10 and 9 percent of the world's population. North America and Oceania with 361 million and 41 million, respectively, together contain only 5 percent of the world's population and enjoy a low degree of population density [5] (see Table 1.2). The two most populous countries of the world, namely China (1.45 billion) and India (1.35 billion), astonishingly account for almost 40 percent of the human population. Based on these observations, we understand that the world's population is distributed lopsidedly in such a way that the low-income Asian and African countries account for the largest populations and have the highest demographic densities. By contrast, the high-income countries of Europe and North America are scarcely populated and have the lowest level of demographic density. An important observation is that many of high-income countries have been witnessing very low fertility rates and high life expectancies for the past seven decades [6]. On the contrary, developing countries are still experiencing high fertility rates combined with improving life expectancy and declining infant mortality. It is shocking to note that the least developed countries have the highest fertility rates around 4.3 children per woman (in 2010 to 2015) and the fastest growth rates estimated about 2.4 percent per year [5]. The general pattern is that the population growth rates across the world are inversely associated with the levels of socioeconomic development. The poorest and the least developed regions (mainly the Sub-Saharan Africa and Indian subcontinent) have the highest population growth rates. Another important disparity between the rich and the poor countries resides in their median age levels, as they represent respectively older and younger populations. For instance, Europe with a median age of 42 years in 2015 has the oldest population, while the median age in many developed countries is estimated around 20 years. In 2015, 24 percent of the European population was aged 60 years or over, whereas the portion of the population over 60 in Latin America and the Caribbean was 11 percent, in Asia it hovered around 12 percent, and in Africa it was only 5 percent [5].

The Diverging Growth Rates: Sub-Saharan Africa and India Are the Fastest Growing Areas

The global population is expected to grow in the next five decades, but there are significant disparities across the world (see Figure 1.2). Those countries with lower median age levels are poised to have the highest population growth in coming years. Africa has the highest growth rate

Table 1.2 *Distribution of the world's population by region*

Region	Population (2017)	Yearly change (%)	Net change	Migrants (net)	Fertility rate	Median age	Urban population (%)	World share (%)
Asia	4,478,315,164	0.95	42,090,691	–1,256,133	2.2	30	49.30	59.60
Africa	1,246,504,865	2.50	30,375,050	–579,959	4.71	19	40.50	16.60
Europe	739,207,742	0.05	358,740	824,644	1.6	42	74.50	9.80
Latin America and the Caribbean	647,565,336	1.02	6,536,030	–414,767	2.15	29	79.70	8.60
Northern America	363,224,006	0.75	2,694,682	1,235,878	1.86	38	82.80	4.80
Oceania	40,467,040	1.42	565,685	190,337	2.42	33	70.80	0.50

Source: www.worldometers.info

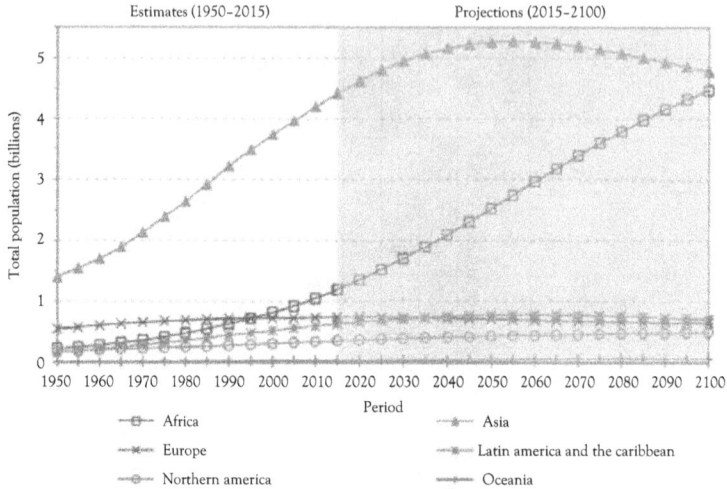

Figure 1.2 Population growth by region, 1950–2100

Source: United nations, department of economic and social affairs. Population Division 2017. World Population Prospects: The 2017 Revision. New York: United Nations.

at 2.5 percent while Europe has the lowest growth rate at 0.04 percent [4]. This high rate of population growth in Africa means that the African population is expected to double in the next 28 years. Based on similar projections, more than half of the global population growth in the next four decades will occur in Africa. Between now and 2100, the populations of many African countries are expected to increase at least three- to fourfold. The populations of extremely poor African countries such as Angola, Burundi, the Democratic Republic of the Congo, Malawi, Mali, Niger, Somalia, Uganda, the United Republic of Tanzania, and Zambia are projected to increase fivefold by 2100 [5]. Nigeria may surpass the United States to become the world's third populous country by 2050. Simply put, 1.3 billion people will be added only in Africa between now and 2050 while Asia and mainly India are responsible for an increase of another billion people for the same period. Based on similar forecasts, the drastic population growth in Africa, unlike Asia, will continue even after 2050 [5]. Consequently, Sub-Saharan Africa's share of global population is projected to grow to 25 percent by 2050 and 39 percent by 2100, while the share of the people residing in Asia will fall to 54 percent by 2050 and 44 percent by 2100.

China (approximately 1.4 billion) and India (approximately 1.3 billion), the two most populous countries of the world, respectively account for 19 and 18 percent of the global population but they are on radically different paths. Unlike China, the fertility rate in India has remained very high (see Table 1.3). As a result, India is supposed to overtake China as the world's most populous country sometime between 2020 and 2025. Consistent with the same estimates, India's population will reach 1.5 billion in 2030 and 1.7 billion in 2050, while the population of China is expected to remain constant until the 2030s and decrease slightly afterward [5]. Northern America, Latin America and the Caribbean, and Oceania are projected to experience smaller population growth levels while Europe is expected to have a population decline by 2050. By 2050, the populations in six countries could exceed 300 million including China, India, Indonesia, Nigeria, Pakistan, and the United States. The population growth in the next decades will be so uneven that nine countries will be responsible for more than half of the world's population surge. These countries include India, Nigeria, Pakistan, the Democratic Republic of the Congo, Ethiopia, the United Republic of Tanzania, the United States, Indonesia, and Uganda. In this club, the only developed country is the United States but the rest represent the developing or poor economies of Asia and Africa.

In sharp contrast to Africa and most parts of Asia, the populations of 48 countries and areas are expected to decline between 2015 and 2050. Many Eastern European countries including Bulgaria, Croatia, Hungary, Latvia, Lithuania, the Republic of Moldova, Romania, Russia, Serbia, and Ukraine, and Japan may experience a sharp population drop of 15 percent or more by 2050 [5, 4]. According to *Financial Times*, Japan's population may decline as much as 31 percent by 2065 and 60 percent by 2115. This means that the population of Japan could plummet from 127 to 88 million by 2065 and to 51 million by 2115 [7]. The population decline in these countries is a result of lower fertility rates and higher median age levels over the course of the past four decades. In the past five years, 83 countries had below-replacement fertility rates while they accounted for 46 percent of the world's population. Currently, the most populous countries with below-replacement fertility, in order of population size, are

Table 1.3 Demographics of the 20 largest countries

Country	Population (2017)	Yearly change (%)	Net change	Density (P/km²)	Land area (km²)	Migrants (net)	Fertility rate	Median age	Urban population (%)	World share (%)
China	1,388,232,693	0.43	5,909,361	148	9,386,293	−360,000	1.55	37	57.60	18.50
India	1,342,512,706	1.18	15,711,130	452	2,973,450	−519,644	2.48	27	32	17.90
The United States	326,474,013	0.73	2,355,226	36	9,144,930	1,001,577	1.89	38	82.10	4.30
Indonesia	263,510,146	1.12	2,929,046	146	1,811,066	−140,000	2.5	28	53.40	3.50
Brazil	211,243,220	0.80	1,675,300	25	8,349,534	3,185	1.82	31	83.50	2.80
Pakistan	196,744,376	2.03	3,917,874	255	770,942	−216,384	3.72	23	38.10	2.60
Nigeria	191,835,936	2.59	4,848,373	211	910,902	−60,000	5.74	18	47.80	2.60
Bangladesh	164,827,718	1.18	1,916,854	1,266	130,175	−445,296	2.23	26	34.50	2.20
Russia	143,375,006	−0.05	−64,826	9	16,292,614	223,577	1.66	39	73.20	1.90
Mexico	130,222,815	1.24	1,590,811	67	1,943,624	−104,717	2.29	27	77.30	1.70
Japan	126,045,211	−0.22	−278,504	346	364,503	70,000	1.4	47	94.30	1.70
Ethiopia	104,344,901	2.45	2,491,633	104	1,000,430	−12,000	4.59	19	19.40	1.40
Philippines	103,796,832	1.51	1,546,699	348	298,181	−140,000	3.04	24	44.20	1.40
Vietnam	95,414,640	1.03	970,440	308	310,090	−40,000	1.96	30	33.80	1.30

GLOBAL DEMOGRAPHIC TRENDS   9

Egypt	95,215,102	1.96	1,831,528	96	994,933	-43,136	3.38	25	39	1.30
Congo	82,242,685	3.16	2,520,061	36	2,265,639	-19,184	6.15	17	38.30	1.10
Iran	80,945,718	1.13	902,572	50	1,628,686	-60,000	1.75	30	73.40	1.10
Germany	80,636,124	-0.06	-46,227	231	348,621	250,000	1.39	46	77.20	1.10
Turkey	80,417,526	1	795,464	105	769,546	400,001	2.1	30	71.20	1.10
Thailand	68,297,547	0.22	150,938	134	510,827	20,000	1.53	38	51	0.90

Source: www.Worldometers.info

China, the United States, Brazil, Russia, Japan, Vietnam, Germany, Iran, and Thailand [5].

Aging Populations: All Areas of the World Are Aging Fast, Except Africa

In most parts of the world including developing countries, we have been observing two important trends: the decline in fertility rates on the one hand and the rise in life expectancy on the other hand. The outcome of these two trends is the emergence of aging populations across the world. Currently, there are around 962 million people aged 60 or over in the world, comprising 13 percent of the global population and growing at a rate of about 3 percent per year [28]. It is projected that, by 2050, half of the global population will reside in countries where at least 20 percent of the inhabitants are aged 60 years or over [8]. The number of people aged 60 and above is expected to double between 2015 and 2050, from 960 million to 2.1 billion globally [5]. Almost 66 percent of this increase will occur in Asia, 13 percent in Africa, 11 percent in Latin America and the Caribbean, and the remaining 10 percent in other regions [5]. Similarly, the number of the oldest-old or people aged 80 or over may triple by 2050 and increase more than sevenfold by the end of the century. This means that the number of people aged 80 or over is projected to increase from 125 million in 2015 to 434 million in 2050 and to 1 billion in 2100 [5].

The pace of population aging is accelerating, but it is not uniform across the globe. Europe and many developed countries such as Japan have been aging for decades; however, the newly industrialized countries such as South Korea have entered the aging phase more recently. In 2015, elderly people comprise 22 percent of the population of high-income countries, 13 percent of upper middle-income countries, 8 percent of lower middle-income countries, and 5 percent of low-income countries [8]. Europe, with a median age of 42 years, has the oldest population, which is expected to reach 46 years by 2050. By contrast, the median age for much of developing countries is hovering around 20 years and may reach 26 years in 2050. Therefore, it is possible to project that the older populations in developed countries will grow in size, but at a much slower pace than those in newly developed countries of Asia and Latin America. In the next two decades, upper middle-income countries are expected to continue to experience a rapid growth in the number of old people. Several upper middle-income countries are projected to become as aged as many of today's high-income countries within the next 15 years. In many developing countries, population aging is taking place much more rapidly than it did in the countries that developed earlier. For example, it took 115 years for France, for the proportion of the population aged 60 years or over to increase from 7 to 14 percent [9]. In contrast, it is estimated that for Brazil it will take just 25 years for the percentage of older people to rise from 7 to 14 percent [8]. For that reason, today's developing countries must adapt much more quickly to the aging populations and their necessities. The impact of aging will be particularly noticeable in the case of Asian countries that account for large portions of the world population. For instance, by 2050, two-thirds of the world's older people will live in Asia (see Figure 1.3). As mentioned previously, China and India are on very different paths of demographic change because of their dissimilar age structure and family planning policies. While China is already an aging country, India is still young and will remain so in the next few decades. Latin American and African countries are expected to have younger populations until 2050 as they still have high fertility rates and lower median age levels. Unlike all other regions, Africa is and will remain the youngest region in the forthcoming decades.

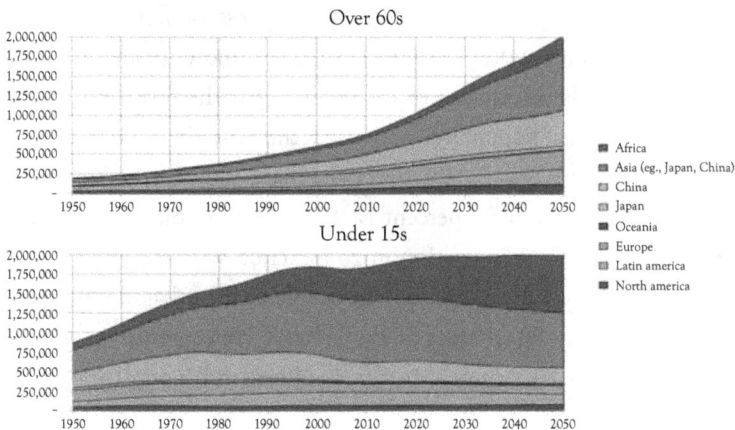

Figure 1.3 *Aging populations growth by region, 1950–2050*

A massive aging population could involve significant implications for the labor market, personal savings, and global productivity. For instance, in Europe and Japan, the social protection systems including health care and pension systems may encounter difficulty in managing their finances [10]. Because of aging populations, disabilities and noncommunicable illnesses such as cardiovascular diseases, cancer, diabetes, and dementia will be rampant, causing financial pressure on public health systems. On the other hand, because of aging populations, many countries may benefit from demographic dividend or a significant boost to their income per capita. As fertility rates decline, the burden of youth dependency reduces, the proportion of workers and savers in the population increases, and women are liberated from childbearing. In an aging society, the existing resources can be allocated to building infrastructure and investing in education and research and development [4]. Indeed, the global aging in most developing countries except in Sub-Saharan Africa is expected to result in lower levels of poverty. Nevertheless, the global aging could slow the pace of economic development in emerging economies particularly in China that will experience a massive shrinking of their workforce in near future. India unlike China will be immune to the effects of population aging, at least for the next two decades.

Urbanization: 2.5 Billion Will Be Urbanized by 2050

Because of the widespread socioeconomic development in the past six decades, the world has gone through a process of fast urbanization. The world's population is constantly becoming more urbanized as cities are attracting a large number of inhabitants. For the first time in 2007, the world's urban population surpassed the world's rural population. According to the World Bank reports, the share of the world's urban population has risen from 30 percent in 1950 to more than 54 percent in 2015. The ongoing urbanization in conjunction with the growth of the global population will add 2.5 billion people to the urban population by 2050, with nearly 90 percent of the increase concentrated in Asia and Africa [11]. By 2050, almost two-thirds of the world's population will live in urban centers [22].

As of 2014, North America and Latin America were the most urbanized regions of the world with over 80 percent urban settlements [25]. In the same year, Europe's rate of urban settlement was close to 73 percent while Africa and Asia were mostly rural with urban settlement rates of 40 and 48 percent, respectively [25]. In 2014, 16 countries still had low levels of urbanization of 20 percent and less, including Burundi, Ethiopia, Malawi, Niger, South Sudan and Uganda in Africa, and Nepal and Sri Lanka in Asia [22]. There are considerable disparities between developed and developing countries with regard to the urbanization process. For instance, most of the developed countries urbanized in the 1960s and 1970s as the urban share of their total populations rose from 47 percent in the 1960s to 60 percent in the early1980s and plateauing subsequently. At present, more than 75 percent of the populations in developing countries still live in rural areas, suggesting that the sharpest increase in the urban centers will happen in such countries [23]. Based on the United Nations estimates, almost 2.5 billion people will be added to the global urban population between 2014 and 2050. Of these 2.5 billion new urban dwellers, almost 90 percent will live in Africa and Asia. Only three countries, namely India, China, and Nigeria, are expected to account for more than one-third of global urban population growth [25]. Seven other countries, notably the Democratic Republic of the Congo, Ethiopia, the United Republic of Tanzania, Bangladesh, Indonesia, Pakistan, and the United States, will account for another 20 percent of the growth of the global urban population [25]. In some Asian countries such as China and Korea, urbanization accompanied economic development, but in many other countries, including Pakistan, Haiti, and the Democratic Republic of the Congo, urbanization happened in the absence of socioeconomic development and despite dysfunctional politics [21]. Indeed, a remarkable trend in the contemporary world is the rapid urbanization in developing and poor nations. For example, in the 1960s, most of the poor nations were rural with urbanization rates over less than 25 percent. In the recent years, the majority of poor countries have urbanized. According to the United Nations, the urbanization rate in developing countries increased from 18 percent in 1950 to 47 percent in 2011 [21].

The urbanization phenomenon has resulted in the emergence of the very large urban centers or "megacities" with more than 10 million people. By 2030, the world is projected to have 41 cities with more than 10 million inhabitants [22]. Currently, 29 megacities are home to 471 million people, an equivalent of 6 percent of the world's total population

[4]. Furthermore, the number of cities with populations over 20 million is increasing fast. In this category, Tokyo (38 million), Delhi (26 million), Shanghai (23 million), Sao Paulo (21 million), Mumbai (21 million), and Mexico City (21 million) are ranked as the largest cities. Several decades ago, most of the world's largest cities were located in the developed countries, but currently large urban centers are found or are being formed in the developing countries of Asia [22] (see Table 1.4.) The megacities involve significant social and economic consequences as some of them like Tokyo (38 million) and Delhi (26 million) are more populous than sizeable countries such as Canada (35 million) and Australia (24 million). The proliferation of such large cities may put a strain on environmental resources including air, water, soil, and ecological systems [4].

Urbanization, particularly in the lower middle-income countries where the pace of urbanization is fastest, may cause substantial socio-economic challenges. Nevertheless, urban centers can offer advantageous services to a large number of people. For instance, health care, education, public transportation, housing, electricity, water, and sanitation are generally available to urban dwellers in a quite effective manner [22]. Populations move to large cities because they are the centers of trade, foreign direct investments, and economic development. Urban dwellers have a better access to larger and more diversified labor markets and enjoy healthier lives. The life expectancy in urban centers is generally higher while the fertility rate is significantly lower. An important pattern is that as countries urbanize their overall total fertility rates decline because the fertility rates in urban centers are much lower than those in rural areas [23].

Global Migration

Demographic trends and international migratory movements are closely correlated. Europe, Northern America, and Australia are net receivers of international migrants because they have lower fertility rates and higher median age levels. On the contrary, Africa, Asia, Latin America, and the Caribbean countries are net senders of international migrants because they have much higher fertility rates and lower median age levels. Between 2000 and 2015, 2.8 million people per year migrated to Europe,

Table 1.4 The 30 largest cities in 2015

Rank	City, country	Population	Rank	City, country	Population	Rank	City, country	Population
1	Tokyo-Yokohama, Japan	37,843,000	11	Sao Paulo, Brazil	20,365,000	21	Buenos Aires, Argentina	14,122,000
2	Jakarta, Indonesia	30,539,000	12	Mexico City, Mexico	20,063,000	22	Tehran, Iran	13,532,000
3	Delhi, India	24,998,000	13	Mumbai, India	17,712,000	23	Istanbul, Turkey	13,287,000
4	Manila, Philippines	24,123,000	14	Osaka-Kobe, Japan	17,444,000	24	Lagos, Nigeria	13,123,000
5	Seoul, South Korea	23,480,000	15	Moscow, Russia	16,170,000	25	Shenzhen, China	12,084,000
6	Shanghai, China	23,416,000	16	Dhaka, Bangladesh	15,669,000	26	Rio de Janeiro, Brazil	11,727,000
7	Karachi, Pakistan	22,123,000	17	Cairo, Egypt	15,600,000	27	Kinshasa, Congo	11,587,000
8	Beijing, China	21,009,000	18	Los Angeles, the United States	15,058,000	28	Tianjin, China	10,920,000
9	New York, the United States	20,630,000	19	Bangkok, Thailand	14,998,000	29	Paris, France	10,858,000
10	Guangzhou-Foshan, China	20,597,000	20	Kolkata, India	14,667,000	30	Lima, Peru	10,750,000

Source: www.Worldometers.info

Northern America, and Oceania [5]. Europe and North America contain 15 percent of the global population but are home to more than half of the world's international migrants [4]. In addition to the diverging demographic trends between developed and developing countries, geopolitical turmoil, war, conflict, and invasion in the Middle East and Asia will contribute to the increasing influx of populations from the poor to the rich countries in the next four decades. The demographic forces are the main drivers of international migration, but the economic factors also have important implications for the direction of migration is always from the less developed and low-income countries to the developed and high-income ones. In the next four decades, the United States, Canada, the United Kingdom, Australia, Germany, the Russian Federation, and Italy are expected to be the top receivers of international migrants [5]. During the same period, Sub-Saharan Africa, India, Bangladesh, China, Pakistan, and Mexico are expected to be the top sources of international migrants. In the current globalized world, skilled and educated migrants are privileged over unskilled and uneducated ones [24]. The international migration flows are affected by multiple constraints set in developed countries' laws. Therefore, in comparison with the historical large-scale migrations, the recent international migratory movements are more selective [24].

It is widely accepted that migration has negative effects on labor supply in developing countries as most of the emigrants come from the educated and skilled workforce [24]. Instead, the sending countries may benefit from the remittances that migrants send back to their countries of origin. Because of increasing economic development in emerging countries, the migration flows from South to North may change to a South-to-South migration pattern. Some emerging countries with high economic growth rates could attract a large number of migrant workers from low-income neighboring countries [12]. Climate change, desertification, destruction of farmland, resource scarcity, air and water pollution, terrorism, and regional conflicts may create new patterns of international migration among the Southern and low-income countries. For example, due to the Syrian conflict, about 3.2 million Syrians have fled their homeland and have migrated to Turkey. The flight of more than 1 million Syrians to Europe in 2015, perhaps one of the largest mass migrations in the recent history, shows that the patterns of international migration are becoming more complex and unpredictable.

Migration is becoming a key contributor to population growth in high-income countries, as the migrants from low-income countries often have higher birth rates than the host population. For example, the average fertility rates of migrants in Europe and the United States are significantly higher than the national averages [13]. Furthermore, by reducing median age levels, migration can indirectly influence the population size and age structure of receiving countries [23]. Migration increases the total dependency ratio of sender countries and reduces their share of working-age population. On the other hand, in receiving countries, migration increases the share of working population and reduces old-age dependency [23].

The Demographics of Faith and Religious Denominations: The Revival of God

The differences in fertility rates and median age levels among the world's major religions are working to change the global religious composition. While many sociologists had predicted the end of religion in the 19th and 20th centuries, it seems that the world as a whole has become more religious in the past four decades. For instance, the share of religious people has grown from 82 percent in 1970 to 88 percent in 2010 and it is expected to increase to 90 percent by 2020. Religiousness is growing mainly due to demographic trends because religious communities have higher fertility rates and procreate more than average. Globally, the number of religiously unaffiliated people, agnostics, and atheists was estimated about 1.1 billion in 2010 [14]. Atheists and other people who do not affiliate with any religion are expected to increase in absolute number particularly in the Western countries such as France, Germany, and the United States, but they will constitute a declining share of the world's population because of the twofold demographic disadvantages of low fertility rates and old-age structures. As a consequence, the share of religiously unaffiliated people is expected to decline from 16 percent in 2010 to 13 percent by 2050 [15].

Currently, Christianity and Islam with respectively 2.2 and 1.6 billion adherents are considered the first and the second largest religious denominations and together account for almost half of the world's population [16] (see Table 1.5). Christianity is and will remain the largest religious

Table 1.5 World major religions

Religious denomination	Share of world population	Population
Christian Catholic 50% Protestant 37% Orthodox 12% Other 1%	31%	2,173,180,000
Muslim Sunni 87%–90% Shia 10%–13%	23%	1,598,510,000
No religion affiliation (atheists and agnostics)	16%	1,126,500,000
Hindu (94% of Hindus live in India)	15%	1,033,080,000
Buddhist (50% of Buddhists live in China)	7%	487,540,000
Folk religionist (faiths associated with a particular group, ethnicity, or tribe)	6%	405,120,000
Other religions (Baha'i, Taoism, Jainism, Shintoism, Sikhism, Tenrikyo, Wicca, Zoroastrianism)	1%	58,110,000
Jew (41% of Jews live in the United States, another 41% in Israel)	0.20%	13,850,000

Source: http://pewforum.org/2012

group in the next four decades, but Islam is growing faster than any other major religion and is expected to overtake Christianity as the largest religious denomination after 2050 [23]. According to the Pew Research projections, the adherents of Christianity are expected to grow but their growth will be slower and they will constitute 35 percent of the global population by 2050 [23]. The Jewish population was estimated about 14 million in 2010 and is expected to reach 16.1 million worldwide by 2050. In the United States, the share of Christians will decline from 75 percent of the population in 2010 to 66 percent in 2050 and Muslims will be more numerous in the United States than the adherents of Judaism will. Unlike all other major religions, the number of Buddhist adherents is

expected to be constant because of low fertility rates and aging populations in countries such as China and Japan. At the same time, the Hindu
population is estimated to surge from 1 to 1.4 billion by 2050 representing an increase of roughly 40 percent. There are important geographic
disparities in the patterns of religious growth in the coming decades. For
example, the religiously unaffiliated population will be concentrated in
Europe and North America and will increase as a share of the population
in these areas. On the other hand, most of the global growth in the number of Muslims and Christians is expected to happen in the low-income
and Sub-Saharan African countries characterized by low median ages and
high fertility rates. Consistent with these estimates, more than 40 percent
of the world's Christians will reside in Sub-Saharan Africa by 2050. The
rapid changes in religious identities may involve important implications
for different spheres of life including politics, the legal system, family,
education, and technology [17, 18]. Furthermore, the growing disparities
among the major religious denominations may lead to cultural collisions,
social or geopolitical tensions, conflicts, and political turmoil.

The Languages of Present and Future

Currently, there are almost 7,000 languages spoken across the world,
but a large number of these languages have limited scopes and some are
facing the risk of disappearance [19]. The linguistic diversity is under
increasing pressure, as 50 to 90 percent of the world's languages are predicted to extinct by the end of 21st century [19]. Because of globalization and advances in telecommunication and transport, the world as a
whole is becoming linguistically and culturally less diverse than ever.
Currently, 15 languages dominate the global stage because they constitute the mother tongues of half of the world's population. At the top
is Mandarin Chinese with almost 1 billion native speakers followed by
Spanish, which is the second most common mother tongue of 500 million people. English is at the third place with over 450 million native
speakers and Hindi and Arabic are at the fourth and fifth places with
almost 300 million native speakers. While the number of native speakers
is an important criterion in determining the power of a language, other
variables such as geography, economy, communication, knowledge, and

media, and diplomacy seem relevant in evaluating the present and future influence of a language. Relying on these criteria, the 10 most dominant languages may be ranked as English, Mandarin, French, Spanish, Arabic, Russian, German, Japanese, Portuguese, and Hindi (see Table 1.6). With an estimated 450 million native speakers, English is considered as the most important language. Indeed, English is the dominant language of the world's largest economy (the United States) and other large economies such as the United Kingdom, Canada, and Australia. English will remain the global lingua franca at least for the next three decades and its native speakers will reach 540 million by 2050. Mandarin is becoming an important language, not only because of a large size of its native speakers but also because of the growing Chinese economy that has become the world's second largest after the United States. While the number of French native speakers is close to 80 million, French is considered as the third influential language of the world because of its geopolitical impact on Africa and its importance in diplomacy and international affairs [27].

It is almost impossible to predict the future of languages, but the power of a language depends highly on the number of its native and foreign speakers. Accordingly, English will remain the most influential language of the world with close to 550 million native speakers at least by 2050. By 2050, there will not be any sizeable growth in the number of native speakers of Mandarin, French, Russian, German, and Japanese. Indeed, these languages belong to countries that because of their socio-economic conditions have very low birth rates and will not experience significant demographic increases. By contrast, the native speakers of languages such as Spanish, Arabic, Hindi, and Portuguese are supposed to have significant growths by 2050. According to a report by the British Council, Hindi, Bengali, Urdu, Indonesian, Spanish, Portuguese, Arabic, and Russian will be some important languages for doing business in the next three decades [20].

References

[1] Lam, D., and M. Leibbrandt. 2013. "Global Demographic Trends and their Implications for Employment." Background Research Paper Submitted to the High-Level Panel on the Post-2015 Development Agenda.

Table 1.6 The most powerful languages

Rank	Score	Language	Native (MM)	Geography	Economy	Communication	Knowledge and Media	Diplomacy
1	0.889	English	446.0	1	1	1	1	1
2	0.411	Mandarin*	960.0	6	2	2	3	6
3	0.337	French	80.0	2	6	5	5	1
4	0.329	Spanish	470.0	3	5	3	7	3
5	0.273	Arabic	295.0	4	9	6	18	4
6	0.244	Russian	150.0	5	12	10	9	5
7	0.191	German	92.5	8	3	7	4	8
8	0.133	Japanese	125.0	27	4	22	6	7
9	0.119	Portuguese	215.0	7	19	13	12	9
10	0.117	Hindi*	310.0	13	16	8	2	10

*If all Chinese dialects/languages (Mandarin being the largest) are considered as one it would not change the rank ordering. However, if Urdu and Hindi—and all the Hindi dialects—are taken as one it would vault it past Portuguese and Japanese.

Source: http://kailchan.ca/2017/05/the-worlds-most-powerful-languages/

[2] Lee, R. 2003. "The Demographic Transition: Three Centuries of Fundamental Change." *The Journal of Economic Perspectives* 17, no. 4, pp. 167–90.

[3] Lam, D. 2011. "How the World Survived the Population Bomb: Lessons from 50 Years of Extraordinary Demographic History." *Demography* 48, no. 4, pp. 1231–62.

[4] Bloom, D.E. 2016. "Demographic Upheaval." *Finance and Development* 53, no. 1, pp. 6–11.

[5] United Nations, Department of Economic and Social Affairs, Population Division 2015. "World Population Prospects: The 2015 Revision, Key Findings and Advance Tables." Working Paper No. ESA/P/WP.241.

[6] Parkes, R. 2015. "The European Union and the Geopolitics of Migration." UI Paper no. 1/2015.

[7] Japan's Population Set to Fall to 88m by 2065. Accessed on June 18, 2017, https://ft.com/content/00df659e-1dcf-11e7-a454-ab04428977f9

[8] Nations, U. 2013. World Population Aging 2013. Department of Economic and Social Affairs PD.

[9] Kinsella, K.G., and Y.J. Gist. 1995. Older Workers, Retirement, and Pensions: A Comparative International Chartbook (No. 95). US Department of Commerce, Economics and Statistics Administration, Bureau of the Census.

[10] European Commission, European Union. 2015. European Strategy and Policy Analysis System. Global Trends to 2030: Can the EU Meet the Challenges Ahead?

[11] United Nations, Department of Economic and Social Affairs, Population Division 2014. "World Urbanization Prospects: The 2014 Revision, Highlights." (ST/ESA/SER.A/352).

[12] Zmud, J., L. Ecola, P. Phleps, and I. Feige. 2013. *The Future of Mobility*. Santa Monica, CA: RAND Corporation.

[13] Andersson, G. 2004. "Childbearing After Migration: Fertility Patterns of Foreign-Born Women in Sweden." *International Migration Review* 38, no. 2, pp. 747–74.

[14] Hackett, C., P. Connor, M. Stonawski, V. Skirbekk, M. Potancoková, and G. Abel. 2015. *The Future of World Religions: Population Growth Projections, 2010–2050*. Washington, DC: Pew Research Center.

[15] Hackett, C., M. Stonawski, M. Potančoková, B.J. Grim, and V. Skirbekk. 2015. "The Future Size of Religiously Affiliated and Unaffiliated Populations." *Demographic Research* 32, p. 829.

[16] Johnson, T., G.A. Bellofatto, A.W. Hickman, B.A. Coon, P.F. Crossing, M. Krause, and J. Yen. 2013. *Christianity in its Global Context, 1970–2020: Society, Religion, and Mission*. Southhampton, MA: Center for the Global Study of Christianity.

[17] Zuckerman, P. 2009. "Atheism, Secularity, and Well-Being: How the Findings of Social Science Counter Negative Stereotypes and Assumptions." *Sociology Compass* 3, no. 6, pp. 949–71. doi:10.1111/j.1751-9020.2009.00247.x

[18] Funk, C., and G. Smith. 2012. *"Nones" on the Rise: One-in-Five Adults have No Religious Affiliation*. Washington, DC: Pew Research Center.

[19] Romaine, S. 2015. "The Global Extinction of Languages and its Consequences for Cultural Diversity." In *Cultural and Linguistic Minorities in the Russian Federation and the European Union*, 31–46. Springer International Publishing.

[20] Noack, R. 2015. The Future of Language. *The Washington Post*. Accessed on August 20, 217, https://washingtonpost.com/news/worldviews/wp/2015/09/24/the-future-of-language/?utm_term=.eec17bd2e40f (accessed August 20, 2017).

[21] Glaeser, E.L. 2014. "A World of Cities: The Causes and Consequences of Urbanization in Poorer Countries." *Journal of the European Economic Association* 12, no. 5, pp. 1154–99.

[22] Population Division 2014. World Urbanization Prospects: The 2014 Revision, Highlights (ST/ESA/SER.A/352). United Nations, Department of Economic and Social Affairs.

[23] Winthrop, R., G. Bulloch, P. Bhatt, and A. Wood. 2015. "Development Goals in an Era of Demographic Change." Global Monitoring Report, 2016.

[24] Gunter, B.G., and R. Hoeven. 2004. "The Social Dimension of Globalization: A Review of the Literature." *International Labour Review* 143, nos. 1–2, pp. 7–43.

[25] The United Nations, Department of Economics and Social Affairs. http://un.org/en/development/desa/population/publications/factsheets/index.shtml

[26] Roser, M., and E. Ortiz-Ospina. 2017. "World Population Growth." Published online at Our WorldInData.org. Retrieved on May 29, 2017.

[27] Population Division 2017. World Urbanization Prospects: The 2017 Revision. United Nations, Department of Economic and Social Affairs.

CHAPTER 2

Globalization: Trends and Consequences

1. Different Views on Globalization
2. Globalization and the Changing Role of Nation-States
3. A New Balance of Economic Power
4. Pressure on Wages, Employment, and Social Welfare
5. Living in an Age of Insecurity and Uncertainty
6. The Decline of Interstate Wars and the Rise of Intrastate Conflicts
7. Time-Space Compression

Different Views on Globalization

Globalization can be defined as a process resulting in more interdependence and mutual awareness among economic, political, and social units of the world [2, 1, 3, 4]. Globalization is a complex and multifaceted phenomenon that is associated with increasing cross-national movements of goods, services, capital, people, and information [1, 2]. Because of its complex nature, globalization is not consensual rather it is accompanied by intense conflicts among various social groups, states, and hegemonic powers [5]. As such, it constitutes an array of interconnections that transcend the borders of nation-states and local communities. Globalization creates conditions through which the events, decisions, and activities in one part of the world cause significant consequences in other parts [6]. It breaks the traditional relationships between territoriality and authority and moves authority from the state and local levels to the universal levels [7]. Consequently, globalization enables us to operate in a network society and interact with each other in real time on a planetary scale regardless of our temporal and spatial constraints.

The origin of globalization can be found in ancient times, but the modern usage of the terminology is associated with the rapid socio-technological transformations of the late 20th century [2, 1] (see Table 2.1). Historically, the end of the Cold War coincided with the beginning of globalization, but it is not clear whether there is a causal relationship between these two phenomena [8]. We might speculate that the end of the Cold War and the subsequent détente between the United States and the Soviet Union created better opportunities for international trade and exchange of ideas. From an economic standpoint, globalization is a significant shift toward an economic system that is no longer based on independent national economies but on a global marketplace for production, distribution, and consumption [9, 10]. Economic globalization is particularly characterized by a sequence of events including liberalization and deregulation of markets, privatization of assets, financial deregulation, cross-national production, and the integration of capital markets [11].

From a cultural standpoint, globalization can be viewed as an increasing convergence in the world's cultural values leading to homogenization of all human societies, irrespective of their historical roots (see Table 2.1). In the past five decades, almost all countries have been witnessing significant socioeconomic transformations marked by state centralization,

Table 2.1 The multiple views on globalization, their meanings, features, and consequences

Perspective	Central idea	Features and consequences
Economic	A global marketplace for production, distribution, and consumption	Liberalization and deregulation of markets Privatization of assets Financial deregulation Cross-national production Integration of capital markets
Cultural	An increasing convergence in the world's cultural values.	Homogenization of all cultural values Prevalence of modernization Acceptance of capitalism and liberal democracy
Socio-technological	A connection of the local communities together so they can function in a coherent planetary system	Unprecedented explosion of information, products, and services Reconciliation between the local and global
Business	Glocalization of business activities	Reproduction of international businesses on a regional or local basis
Sociological	A compression of temporal and spatial dimensions	Dialectical linkage of distant localities Reflexivity

urbanization, universal education, and higher levels of literacy. According to this view, globalization characterizes a prevalence of modernization, a homogenization of values around the principles of capitalism and liberal democracy and, more recently, an acceptance of American version of Enlightenment that ultimately is leading to the McDonaldization of society [12]. Furthermore, globalization can be seen as a social revolution driven by technological advances that eventually transform the globe into a single market [12]. According to Manuel Castells [2], globalization connects the local communities together so they can function in a coherent planetary system. In the recent decades, we are witnessing a paradigmatic shift in the way we think about a variety of social and economic relations [12]. An extensive shake-up of economic activities at the regional and local levels is happening and an unprecedented explosion of information, products, and services is sweeping across the planet [12]. As a consequence of these transformations, the global is meeting the local and globalization is becoming glocalization, in other words, a mélange of local and global. From a business standpoint, globalizing corporations are often considered multinational or transnational entities that adopt a "glocalization strategy" to reproduce their businesses on a regional or local basis. Thus, the glocalization strategy allows an international company to become accepted as a local organization while trying not to transfer control to the local subsidiaries.

From a sociological perspective, it is possible to suggest that globalization brings about a compression of temporal and spatial dimensions [13, 14, 43]. This implies that the inhabitants of the globalized world are becoming more and more aware of each other's presence and are communicating and interacting reciprocally. Consistent with this idea, Giddens (1990) emphasizes that globalization is an interactive and dialectical process that links distant localities in such a way that local happenings are shaped by events occurring many miles away and vice versa [14]. Globalization is often described as an unfinished, changeable, and intermittent phenomenon with many contradictory effects and implications [15, 16, 2].

Globalization and the Changing Role of Nation-States

Globalization denationalizes the markets, opens the door to international competition, and eventually pushes nation-states to react to international forces rather than to domestic population. Despite the fact that their sources of legitimacy are chiefly domestic, nation-states become increasingly responsive to the global community [17]. Economic integration empowers international organizations so they can directly decide about the fiscal and monetary policies, trade, tariffs, environmental issues, and interest rates. Globalization restraints nation-states to tax, spend, and control their domestic affairs. Moreover, globalization, by facilitating the cross-border movements of labor and capital, loosens the government control and makes national borders less relevant. In addition to the strong supranational institutions, big businesses and powerful corporations put a lot of pressure on the ability of nation-states to function properly [2]. Nations and their citizens become hostages of supranational markets, international lenders, and investment banks. Globalization creates problems of international governance and cuts the regulatory power of states. It weakens the ability of nation-states to regulate what happens on their own land. Thus, it is plausible to suggest that, by creating a constant tension between national and supranational forces, globalization and the ensuing economic integration undermine the traditional roles of nation-states. The advocates of globalization believe that the economic integration affects the nation-states, but does not destroy them. As a solution, they suggest that the nation-states should become more resilient and agile to benefit from the economic effects of globalization. Some go further and argue that nation-states should not fear globalization, as the global forces ultimately serve the interests of citizens. This argument advocates that globalization is a continuation of capitalist development; therefore, those nation-states that become more globalized are more likely to become prosperous and successful.

Regardless of the perspective that we adopt, it is obvious that globalization undermines the traditional functions of the nation-state, particularly in the case of smaller countries that do not have abundant financial resources and large populations. Furthermore, the large multinational corporations and many other global institutions such as the International Monetary Fund (IMF), the World Trade Organization (WTO), and the World Bank are not restrained by any democratic legitimacy or social accountability. The financial crises in Greece and Ireland showed that the smaller nation-states are incapable of exerting their sovereign rights during financial hardship or extended periods of distress, rather they become fully dependent on supranational institutions to avoid the risk of collapse.

The aforementioned discussion leads us to three important conclusions. First, the effects of globalization on nation-states are mainly inevitable because these effects are the direct consequences of temporal and spatial compression. Second, globalization and economic integration often serve the interests of nation-states. The more globalized nation-states are generally more successful, powerful, and prosperous. Therefore, globalization might change the role of nation-states, but it does not necessarily undermine their power. Third, we can assume that, in the game of globalization, some nation-states will be winners as they gain power and influence while others could be labeled as losers as they continue to decline. In addition to these three conclusions, we should keep in mind that the changing role of nation-states offers an opportunity for the creation of a system of global governance where important issues such as environmental degradation, climate change, overpopulation, and international security can be effectively tackled.

A New Balance of Economic Power

Globalization of trade and production has led to a surge in the worldwide wealth over the past three decades. The world output (gross world product) has tripled in the 20 years between 1988 and 2008. Despite the financial crisis of 2007 to 2008, the global trade has risen more than 50 percent in the last decade [18]. More developing countries are embarked on international business. Currently, the South–South commercial relations mark more than 30 percent of the global trade. In merchandise, the South–South trade is almost equal to North–North trade [19]. The cross-border value chains and operations are becoming so popular that a large fraction (almost 56 percent) of global trade is devoted to intermediate or unfinished products [20]. As globalization is easing the cross-national movements of capital, people, technology, and merchandise, the global economy is witnessing significant changes and a new balance of economic power is being formed. While the economists and trade theorists emphasize that trade is not a zero-sum game, it appears that there are some apparent winners and losers in the globalization game. In the early decades of the 20th century, only a couple of Western countries namely the United States, Britain, France, Germany, and the Netherlands dominated the arena of international trade [21]. In the past four decades, the dominance of the Western countries has been challenged by the rise of many southern countries, notably China, South Korea, South Africa, and India (see Figure 2.1). For instance, the share of the United States of the world's output has fallen from 27.3 percent in the 1950s to 18 percent in 2008, while for the same period the share of China of the world's output has risen drastically from 4.6 to 17.5 percent. China's growth is an essential feature of globalization. China grew from 5 percent of global gross domestic product (GDP) in 1978 to 17 percent in 2011 and may become the world's largest economy at some point within the next 15 years [22]. By 2018, it is expected that the shares of Japan and the European Union (EU) of the world GDP fall to 6 and 20 percent, respectively, while those of China, ASEAN (Association of South East Asian Nations), and Latin America are expected to rise to 15.3, 3.3, and 8.3 percent, respectively. The impact of globalization on the wealth of individuals in the southern countries is particularly noteworthy. For instance, in the past 30 years GDP per capita in China has risen from a tiny $314 in 1990 to more than

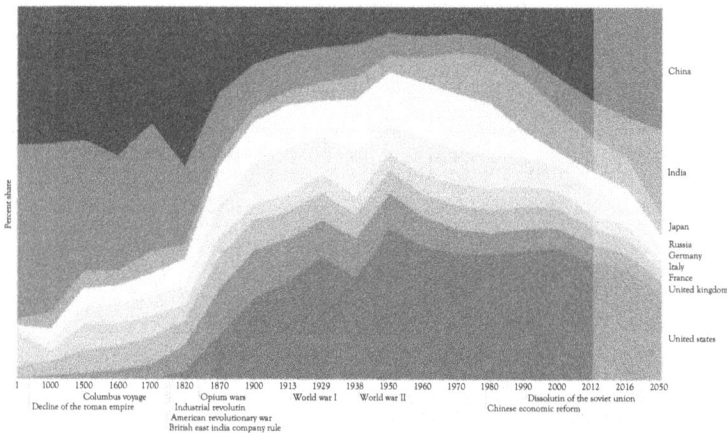

Figure 2.1 **A new balance of economic power: Past, present, and future (based on share of combined GDP of nine countries)**

Sources: GDP data for years 1–2000: Angus Maddison, University of Groningen; 2016 IMF-projected GDP growth; 2050 PricewaterhouseCoopers-projected GDP growth.

$6,000 in 2012 [23]. Even in Sub-Saharan Africa, the GDP per capita has climbed from $627 in 2004 to $1,349 in 2012. The growth of emerging economies, in particular, China and India, is radically changing the distribution of global economic power. Based on some projections, the OECD (Organisation for Economic Co-operation and Development) countries may constitute a minority of the world economy by 2030. Globalization implies the increasing interdependence of the world's economies; therefore, it may rebalance the distribution of wealth across the world leading to the resurgence of China, India, and many other emerging countries with sizeable populations and resources. As Eastern and Southern countries are rising, they become more assertive and claim more space on the world stage vis-à-vis big global players at the top of the pyramid. The developed countries of Western Europe and North America are required to make severe and often painful structural adjustments that often lead to the popular discontent of their citizens. In the recent years, the right wing and populist movements are gaining momentum as they are taking advantage of the popular dissatisfaction with globalization and push their agenda in favor of more interventionist and protectionist economic policies. It seems that as Western countries are losing their traditional economic dominance and privileges, their domestic affairs are adversely affected.

Pressure on Wages, Employment, and Social Welfare

Globalization of production means that multinational corporations scatter their value chain activities across the world to maximize the location advantages including labor, natural resources, and technology. With the advent of new telecommunication technologies in the 1990s, there was a massive departure of manufacturing companies from the industrialized countries to the Asian developing countries. The sudden shift to low-cost countries caused massive unemployment and underemployment in the manufacturing sector in many industrialized countries and stressed the workers' compensation levels. Since then, American workers employed in the industries in direct competition with low-cost imports have seen job dislocation and sliding wage pressures [24]. At the same time, a significant drop in domestic revenues collected from lower tariffs and lower corporate taxes led many governments to cut on social protection programs, and thus strained unskilled or semiskilled workers even more. Under such budgetary pressures, many national governments in the western countries have cut their spending in social protection programs, including pension plans, unemployment, and child care [25]. European countries remained mainly reluctant to wage reduction, maintained their social protection programs, and emphasized equitable income distribution. Not surprisingly, under the pressure of the global forces, most of the European countries namely France, Spain, and Italy have lost their labor competitiveness and have shown higher unemployment levels in the recent years. Globalization in the United States has resulted in higher wage gaps, stagnant income, but relatively lower levels of unemployment than Europe [30, 26]. The negative effects of outsourcing on the wage levels are particularly significant in the case of low-skilled manufacturing workers implying that they are the real losers of globalization. By contrast, the globalization of production does not cause negative implications for high-skilled workers as they are mainly immune to outsourcing and even may benefit from it [27]. The impacts of globalization in developing countries are very different. Indeed, a few emerging countries have essentially benefited from the globalization, but a large number of nations that do not have reliable political, legal, economic, and social institutions have been left behind and in some cases have lost their manufacturing and even their agricultural industries. Joseph Stiglitz, an American economist and a professor at Columbia University, [28] suggests that globalization and the subsequent economic liberalization in developing countries that do not have adequate economic institutions may hurt both employment and productivity.

Living in an Age of Insecurity and Uncertainty

By making the national borders less relevant and by compressing time and space, globalization has created higher levels of economic, political, and technological risk. The sociologists Ulrich Beck and Anthony Giddens coined the term "risk society" to emphasize the risky nature of globalization era [29]. Similarly, Zygmunt Bauman uses the term "liquidity" to illustrate the uncertainty and riskiness of a globalized world. According to

Beck (1992), globalization is essentially an uncertain phenomenon that increases social insecurity: it undermines the territoriality and sovereignty of the nation-state, weakens its authority, and compromises economic stability by prioritizing the whims of financial markets and international speculators [17]. The risks associated with globalization and economic integration are various: unemployment and underemployment, food supply contamination, mass migration, identity crises, terrorism, fundamentalism, cultural and racial clashes, financial instability, market turmoil, currency war, cyber-attacks, industrial espionage, computer snooping, compromised privacy, environmental degradation, health problems, and pandemics [30, 31]. For instance, the growth of international trade and movement of people may spread communicable diseases around the world. Globalization is believed to have very negative implications for the natural environment. As emerging countries strive to attract more foreign capital and production, they turn a blind eye on the environment. Under these circumstances, the multinational corporations of Western nations rush to set up production facilities in the emerging countries to take advantage of their lenient environmental regulations [32]. The neo-liberal policies of a globalized economy facilitate the privatization and monetization of natural resources and mines, and thus provide big multinationals the opportunity to maximize their profits to the detriment of local communities. Globalization risks affect all the humanity, but the poor are particularly vulnerable, as they do not have sufficient resources to withstand the tumultuous times when markets collapse, economies contract, and jobs are lost.

Furthermore, since globalization increases exposure of people to foreign cultures, it can cause collisions among racially, culturally, or religiously distinct members of our societies. The movements of people across the globe lead to multicultural or heterogeneous societies whose members suffer from identity crisis. Globalization and its multiple technological artifacts create a standard universal culture that destroys the existing traditions, values, and patterns of communication and thus brings about new types of risk and uncertainty [32]. The effects of globalization on culture are paradoxical because it seeks to homogenize cultural values on the one hand, but it also increases awareness of cultural heterogeneity on the other hand. International marketing and communications pave the way for the mass import of various American materials including food, clothing, music, films, books, and television programs that ultimately change the traditional and religious cultural values in conservative societies [9]. As the traditional and religious groups feel threatened by the globalized values, they confront all manifestations of globalization particularly the American artifacts and symbols. In the extreme cases, the encounter between global cultural flows and inherited local identities leads to a bitter conflict between two opposite worldviews: "McWorld" and "Jihad" [9, 33].

The Decline of Interstate Wars and the Rise of Intrastate Conflicts

By creating interdependence among trade partners, globalization could deter the interstate military conflicts. After the Second World War, the number of interstate wars has dropped despite the fact that the number of states in the international community has tripled [34]. Obviously, the decline in the occurrence of interstate conflicts may be attributed to other factors including the deterrent effect of nuclear weapons and the success of many liberal democracies and free-market economies across the world. Nevertheless, the key role of globalization and economic exchange in establishing and maintaining peace cannot be denied. It has been suggested that countries with more extensive economic relations are likely to have higher opportunity costs from escalation to war. Such countries are more likely to reach resolution via diplomacy and negotiation. Simply put, if "war is the continuation of politics by other means" [44], the globalized states are less likely to choose it. The EU is the prime example of a globalized project that was designed to maintain peace and prosperity across Europe. That is why the 2012 Nobel Peace Prize was awarded to the EU for its contribution to the advancement of peace and reconciliation in Europe for the past six decades. The decline of direct and interstate conflicts has led to an increased incidence of other types of conflict such as proxy wars, intrastate flights, asymmetrical warfare, and terrorist attacks. The share of irregular fights is estimated at 80 percent of all conflicts. In the past 15 years, we have been witnessing the formation of multiple proxy wars, namely in Syria, Libya, Afghanistan, Ukraine, Yemen, and Iraq where opposing states prefer indirect war via proxy groups rather than full-fledged and classical confrontations. Taliban, Al-Qaeda, and the Islamic State of Iraq and Syria (ISIS) are the well-known examples of terrorist groups that have appeared in the past 15 years. These terrorist groups fight on the behalf of the states that do not want to enter an inter-state war directly. Among them, ISIS exemplifies how a terrorist group can grow thanks to globalization and new technologies. Indeed, the ISIS has been extremely effective in utilizing the Internet and social media to hire new members, raise funds, organize terrorist operations, and disseminate its propaganda across the globe.

Time-Space Compression

Globalization changes the most fundamental divisions in our social relations including the distinctions between local and global, proximity and distance, domestic and foreign, and national and international. Because of the innovative telecommunication and transport technologies, global events take place nearly simultaneously anywhere and everywhere in the world [35]. Globalization allows the geographically distant events and actions to increasingly impact on the local conditions. By intensifying, multiplying, and accelerating social relations, globalization reduces the spatial and temporal distances [36]. This dual time-space compression is an essential feature of globalization that implies some important consequences.

According to Harvey (1989), capitalism attempts to eliminate all spatial barriers and annihilate space through time [37] (see Figure 2.2). The impetus to the annihilation of barriers results in a tempo-spatial compression suggesting that the world is experienced socially and materially as a smaller place [38]. For instance, multinational corporations increasingly rely on new technologies of telecommunication to disperse their business activities across the world and take advantage of location endowments such as cheap labor, abundant resources, sizeable markets, and fiscal rewards. Therefore, the large and even midsized businesses do not belong to a specific location or a nation anymore, rather they are becoming liquid entities that evolve beyond the limits of time and space. For them, the social space as a geographically recognizable location no longer exists.

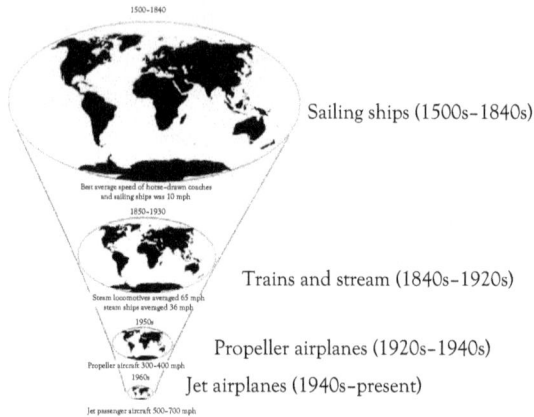

Figure 2.2 Time-space compression

Source: Harvey (1990) [39].

Hence, globalization brings about deterritorialization process implying that various social activities occur regardless of the location of participants. Globalization transforms the social world by linking together and expanding human activities across regions and continents [1]. As a consequence of the tempo-spatial compression, economic production is accelerated through processes such as vertical disintegration and just-in-time delivery. The accelerated economic production in its turn leads to an acceleration of financial exchange and consumption [38, 39]. Especially, globalization is marked by a shift from an economy based on the manufacturing of industrial goods by low-skilled workers to one based on the creation of more ephemeral informational goods and services by knowledge workers [40, 41]. This "global informational capitalism" creates the different organizational forms that drastically change our relationship with our environment. The new information technologies make it necessary to reorganize businesses into global webs operating efficiently, abolishing constraints of space and time [40, 42]. The global workplace becomes a virtual place or a "nonspace" where the constraints of space, social organization, and local institutional arrangements are eliminated or weakened. In this globalized world, the geographical distance is dead and a new virtual social space has emerged that is controlled by capitalists, traders, and managers. They are using high-speed around-the-world and around-the-clock technologies in cyberspace to run their businesses. The global workplace is stripped off from its temporal and spatial contexts and becomes a universal space for communication and innovation among employees [40, 43, 42]. Inherent in the tempo-spatial compression is the increasing velocity of social activity that is driven by the proliferation of high-speed transportation, telecommunication, and information technologies in the past three decades after the 1970s. Indeed, the interconnectedness of social relations and the compression of time and space hinge upon the fast movement of people, information, capital, and merchandise across the world. According to Harvey (1989), in a globalized society capital moves at a pace faster than before, as the production, circulation, and exchange of capital happen at increasing speeds. In the absence of a high social velocity, the compression of time and space seems impossible.

References

[1] Held, D., A. McGrew, D. Goldblatt, and J. Perraton. 1999. *Global Transformations*. Stanford, CA: Stanford University Press.

[2] Guillén, M.F. 2001. "Is Globalization Civilizing, Destructive or Feeble? A Critique of Five Key Debates in the Social Science Literature." *Annual Review of Sociology* 27, no. 1, pp. 235–60.

[3] Petrella, R. 1996. "Globalization and Internationalization." *States Against Markets: The Limits of Globalization*, pp. 62–83.

[4] Steger, M.B. 2010. *Globalization*, 63. John Wiley & Sons, Ltd.

[5] Santos, B.D.S. 2002. "The Processes of Globalisation." *Revista Crítica de Ciências Sociais and Eurozine*, pp. 1–48.

[6] McGrew, A. 1990. "A Global Society." In *Modernity and Its Futures*, eds. S. Hall, D. Held and A. McGrew.

[7] Cerny, P.G. 1997. "Paradoxes of the Competition State: The Dynamics of Political Globalization." *Government and Opposition* 32, no. 2, pp. 251–74.

[8] Reich, S. 1998. *What Is Globalization?: Four Possible Answers*, 261 vols. Helen Kellogg Institute for International Studies.

[9] Lerche III, C.O. 1998. "The Conflicts of Globalization." *International Journal of Peace Studies* 3, no. 1, pp. 47–66.

[10] Holm, H.H., and G. Sørensen. 1995. *Whose World Order?: Uneven Globalization and the End of the Cold War*. Westview Pr.

[11] Jones, R.B. 2013. *Globalisation and Interdependence in the International Political Economy: Rhetoric and Reality*. Bloomsbury Publishing.

[12] Carnoy, M., M. Castells, S. Cohen, and F.H. Cardoso. 1993. *The New Global Economy in the Informational Age: Reflections on Our Changing World*. Penn State Press.

[13] Harvey, D. 1999. "Time-Space Compression and the Postmodern Condition." *Modernity: Critical Concepts* 4, pp. 98–118.

[14] Giddens, A. 1990. "The Consequences of Modernity Cambridge." *Polity* 53, no. 83, pp. 245–60.

[15] Giddens, A. 2000. *Runaway World: How Globalization is Reshaping Our Lives.* New York: Routledge.

[16] Gilpin, R. 2000. *The Challenge of Global Capitalism.* Princeton, NJ: Princeton University Press.

[17] Jarvis, D.S. 2007. "Risk, Globalisation and the State: A Critical Appraisal of Ulrich Beck and the World Risk Society Thesis." *Global Society* 21, no. 1, pp. 23–46.

[18] Grevi, G., D. Keohane, B. Lee, and P. Lewis. 2013. *Empowering Europe's Future: Governance, Power, and Options for the EU in a Changing World.* The European Union.

[19] Grevi, G., D. Keohane, B. Lee, and P. Lewis. 2013. *Empowering Europe's Future: Governance, Power, and Options for the EU in a Changing World.* The European Union.

[20] Miroudot, S., R. Lanz, and A. Ragoussis. 2009. Trade in Intermediate Goods and Services.

[21] Baldwin, R.E., and P. Martin. 1999. *Two Waves of Globalisation: Superficial Similarities, Fundamental Differences (No. w6904).* National Bureau of Economic Research.

[22] Maddison, A. 2008. *Historical Statistics for the World Economy: 1-2006 AD.* Conference Board and Groningen Growth and Development Centre, Total Economy Database.

[23] Fukuyama, F. June 2013. "The Middle Class Revolution." *Wall Street Journal.*

[24] Bivens, J. 2007. "Globalization, American wages, and inequality." The Past, Present, and Future, Economic Policy Institute. Working Paper, 279.

[25] Benvenisti, E., and G. Nolte. 2004. *The Welfare State, Globalization, and International Law.* Springer Science & Business Media.

[26] Stiglitz, J.E. 2003. *The Roaring Nineties: A New History of the World's Most Prosperous Decade.* New York, NY: W.W. Norton & Company.

[27] Geishecker, I., and H. Görg. 2004. *International Outsourcing and wages: Winners and Losers.* Manuscript, DIW Berlin.

[28] Stiglitz, J.E. 2005. "More Instruments and Broader Goals: Moving Toward the Post-Washington Consensus." In *Wider Perspectives on Global Development,* 16–48. UK: Palgrave Macmillan.

[29] Beck, U. 1992. *Risk Society: Towards a New Modernity,* 17 vols. Sage.

[30] Gunter, B.G., and R. Hoeven. 2004. "The Social Dimension of Globalization: A Review of the Literature." *International Labour Review* 143, nos. 1–2, pp. 7–43.

[31] Scheve, K., and M.J. Slaughter. 2004. "Economic Insecurity and the Globalization of Production." *American Journal of Political Science* 48, no. 4, pp. 662–74.

[32] Khan, S., and A. Najam. 2009. "The Future of Globalization and Its Humanitarian Impacts." Humanitarian Horizons Project, FIC. https:// wikis. uit. tufts. edu/confluence/display/FIC/The+ Future+ of+ Globalizat ion+ and+ its+ Humanitarian+ Impacts

[33] Fuller, G. 1995. "The Next Ideology." *Foreign Policy* 98, Spring 1995.

[34] Pettersson, T., and P. Wallensteen. 2015. "Armed Conflicts, 1946–2014." *Journal of Peace Research* 52, no. 4, pp. 536–50.

[35] Scholte, J.A. 1996. "The Geography of Collective Identities in a Globalizing World." *Review of International Political Economy* 3, no. 4, pp. 565–607.

[36] Scholte, J.A. 2000. *What is 'Global' About Globalization?*. Macmillan.

[37] Harvey, D. 2000. *Spaces of Hope,* 7 vols. University of California Press.

[38] Oke, N. 2009. "Globalizing Time and Space: Temporal and Spatial Consid-erations in Discourses of Globalization." *International Political Sociology* 3, no. 3, pp. 310–26.

[39] Harvey, D. 1990. *The Condition of Postmodernity*. Oxford: Blackwell Publishing.

[40] O'Riain, S. 2006. "Time-Space Intensification: Karl Polanyi, The Double Movement, and Global Informational Capitalism." *Theory and Society* 35, no. 5, pp. 507–28.

[41] Castells, M. 1997. *The Rise of the Network Society.* Cambridge, MA: Black-well.

[42] Reich, R. 1991. *The Work of Nations.* New York, NY: Vintage.

[43] Giddens, A. 1991. *The Consequences of Modernity.* Oxford: Blackwell.

[44] Clausewitz, C.V. 1984. "On War." Edited and Translated by Howard, Michael, and Paret, Peter.

CHAPTER 3

Culture in the Contemporary World

Convergence, Divergence, and Cultural Mélange

Convergence

In an interconnected world, consumer goods, labor, capital, people, technology, and more importantly ideas travel across borders much faster and easier than ever. The large multinational corporations capitalize on their substantial power to overcome institutional and legal barriers of nation-states. Across the planet, consumers tend to watch the same television programs, listen to the pop music, consume common global brand products and services, and wear the same or similar clothes [1, 2]. The computerized networks facilitate the fast or free movement of information across national boundaries and surmount the limits of geography, language, and ethnicity [3]. These changes gradually push all the world's nations to embrace the value systems of the established Western capitalistic economies. Local communities are affected by powerful cultures, lose their identities, and ultimately become part of a global culture [1, 4]. According to this perspective, globalization leads to cultural convergence as it forces all cultures toward homogeneity without leaving any room for diversities. For Ritzer (2008), cultural convergence is about the

Americanization of local cultures [39, 1, 4]. The Americanization is the dominant version of Western culture that is fueled by the huge socio-economic and technological achievements of the United States in the past century. America is undeniably the dominant culture in telecommunication technology. Some 85 percent of web pages originate from the United States and American businesses control 75 percent of the world's packaged software market [1, 5]. Furthermore, the American culture is central to the global media, entertainment, and music. The homogenization paradigm implies that the global flow of cultural elements takes place in a one-way manner from the Western industrialized countries, mainly from the United States, to the rest of world. For some people in developing countries, the cultural homogenization is a disturbing and even destructive force. It is an assault of global capitalism on their local cultures, religions, traditions, and identities [1, 6, 7, 8].

Divergence

The second perspective on the contemporary world's culture is divergence or heterogeneity. The divergence perspective holds that cultures are in a constant conflict with each other. In a globalized world, people become much more aware of their unique values and take pride in their cultural identities. Globalization makes people aware of their diverse national cultures [9, 1]. The question of "who am I?" gains importance and shapes the sociocultural relations across the world [10]. Since local cultures are the source of identity and pride, people defend them against the perturbing forces of globalization. The intelligentsia in many developing countries complains that globalization does not involve an equitable exchange among the world's nations rather it is a form of cultural imperialism where products, services, and more importantly cultural values from the United States and other Western countries are imposed on the rest of world [12, 11]. They view the changing patterns in consumption, language usage, dress code, human image ideals, education, and sexual behavior as potential threats of globalization to their local cultures and identities. A radical and rapid change of local identities may cause grave psychological and social shocks. For that reason, some local cultures resist the disturbing forces of globalization and tend to protect or even emphasize their traditional values. Based on these arguments, it is possible to suggest that, in addition to cultural convergence, globalization may involve some degrees of cultural divergence.

Cultural Hybridization (Mélange)

The cultural convergence and divergence views respectively ignore the local reception of Western culture and the adaptation of its elements to the local cultures. In fact, the interaction between global and local cultures creates a constant battle between convergence and divergence forces, which ultimately leads to cultural hybridization or cultural mélange [14, 12, 13]. The main idea of cultural hybridization is that some elements of the global culture are adapted to the receiving local cultures and gradually become like the indigenous parts. The new cultures integrate both global and local cultures but are neither the former nor the latter [4]. Therefore, globalization becomes a mixture of convergence and divergence forces leading to a complex cultural mélange [12, 15]. The process of cultural hybridization destabilizes the old-fashioned definitions of ethnicity, localness, and traditional ways of life [1, 16]. Since culture has different layers such as basic assumptions, values, and artifacts, the superficial elements of a culture are more likely to be mixed together, but the deeply rooted values and beliefs are hard to change. Therefore, globalization could bring about the processes of convergence and divergence at the same time representing overlapping socio-techno-cultural landscapes [1, 17]. Cultural hybridization could be beneficial to the humanity, as the richest cultural traditions have often emerged at the meeting points of noticeably different cultures, such as Athens, the Indus Valley, and Mexico [1, 18].

Diversity, Multiculturalism, and the Lack of Social Cohesion

A variety of factors including the advances in telecommunication and transport especially globalization have created opportunities for migration from developing countries to industrialized nations over the course of past four decades. Consequently, many of the Western countries are progressively experiencing higher levels of socio-ethnic, cultural, linguistic, and religious diversity. For example, it is estimated that 8 to 10 percent of the population in France is from the North African descent. The black Africans constitute more than 3.5 percent of the French population. Germany, which has received more than 1 million migrants only in 2016, hosts over 3 million people of Turkish descent. The large cities of the Western Europe and North America, notably London, Paris, Frankfurt, Brussels, Toronto, New York, Los Angeles, and Chicago, consist of extremely diverse ethnicities. According to Canada's *National Post* newspaper, 51 percent of residents in Toronto were born outside Canada [40]. Based on the 2010 United States Census, the populations of people from Indian descent in America grew almost 70 percent between 2000 and 2010 and reached 4 million in 2015 [41]. Due to significant cultural differences between the home and the host countries, a large number of migrants are not fully integrated into their new communities. Some newcomers remain unemployed and marginalized living in segregated ghettos. The marginalized immigrants feel at home neither in their culture of origin nor in the culture to which they have immigrated. On the one hand, they have lost their original culture and, on the other hand, they are not connected to the new culture that they found too different from theirs. Some immigrants experience higher levels of discrimination and feel that their new culture does not accept them because of their distinct race, skin color, ethnicity, religion, or lower socioeconomic status. The greater the cultural distance between the migrants' culture and the host culture, the more likely that marginalization happens. Marginalization may have different forms. For instance, in some cases, the immigrants do not show any commitment to the new culture and stick to their cultures of origin. Occasionally, they lose their culture of origin and do not adopt a new culture. As a result, they may become "cultured," "deterritorialized," or "unrooted" [47, 48].

The lack of integration and the resulting social incoherence may cause tensions between the ethnoreligious minorities and the host countries (see Figure 3.1). Some serious riots erupted in Paris in 2005 and in London in 2011 involving the burning of cars, vandalizing public buildings, and damaging private properties [42, 43, 44]. Similarly, in the United States, there has been a continuous tension between the African Americans and the law enforcement and, on many occasions, violence,

Figure 3.1 Diversity could become a source of social conflict: French police confronting a woman on a beach as part of a controversial ban on the burkini in 2016

Source: https://theguardian.com/world/2016/aug/24

riots, and vandalism have broken out. In 2014, after the fatal shooting of Michael Brown by a white police officer, riots erupted in Ferguson, Missouri, for many weeks causing vandalism, looting, rioting, arson, and gunshots [45]. Different countries have taken different measures to manage cultural and ethnic diversities. A few countries like Canada allow multiculturalism and embrace the coexistence of multiple languages and ethnicities. Some do not recognize the cultural diversity within their borders and others turn a blind eye on diversity or try to deny its existence [19, 49, 50]. Some countries may take drastic measures to assimilate the minorities into the mainstream society [19, 51]. For instance, France emphasizes the cultural and linguistic homogeneity of the society as the cornerstone of the republican ideal where liberty, equality, and fraternity can best be achieved. After all, it seems that these mandatory measures have not been effective in mitigating the pernicious effects of marginalization in France [19].

The Clash of Cultures/Civilizations

The waves of globalization and by extension Westernization have been perturbing all the world's cultures particularly the traditional ones. Globalization is accompanied by the prevalence of modern values such as rationality, secularity, individualism, freedom of speech, and self-expression that are in evident conflict with the traditional values like religiosity, collectivism, and submissiveness to authority [20, 21]. As such, globalization and westernization may lead to cultural anxiety and cultural clash. The forms and scales of the reactions to globalization vary across the world from nuanced and limited resentment to revolution and social turmoil. In much of the Western world including the United States, Europe, Australia, Canada, and Japan where modern values are already dominant, cultural reactions to globalization have been limited or nonexistent. The intelligentsia in some European countries such as France sporadically expresses their concerns about the disruptive effects of globalization on art, music, and literature, but as a whole their public does not consider globalization an existential threat [22]. By contrast, the developing and particularly Islamic countries have shown ambivalent and contradictory attitudes toward globalization, westernization, and the associated cultural consequences. On the one hand, these societies are embracing the global capitalism, are consuming its products, and are benefiting from the subsequent technological innovations. On the other hand, they see the advent of a new era as an existential threat to their traditional values and lifestyles. Truly, many Muslim countries cannot withstand the rapid socioeconomic and cultural changes of globalization and remain desperate in a struggle between tradition and Western secular modernity.

In addition to the constant tension between traditional and global/modern values, the world is prone to significant cultural conflicts at the civilizational fault lines. Samuel Huntington suggested that, after the epochs of colonialism and the Cold War, the world entered a new stage, in which the cultural and civilizational clashes are more likely to happen because the most important divisions among populations become cultural rather than ideological, political, or economic [23]. According to Huntington's famous thesis, the world can be divided into eight major civilizations/cultures as the lasting constitutions of human societies (see Figure 3.2). These eight major civilizations/cultures are demarcated by a combination of religious, linguistic, historical, and geographical factors.

1. Sinic: the common culture of China and Chinese communities in Southeast Asia including Vietnam and Korea.

Figure 3.2 According to Samuel Huntington, the present time is marked by increasing levels of conflict among the world's civilizations, particularly between the Islamic and Western civilizations

2. Japanese: Japanese culture as uniquely different from the rest of Asia.

3. Hindu: identified as the core Indian civilization.

4. Islamic: originating on the Arabian Peninsula and spread across North Africa, Iberian Peninsula, and Central Asia. The Islamic culture includes Arab, Turkic, Persian, and Malay subdivisions.

5. Orthodox: the culture centered in Russia that is separate from Western Christianity.

6. Western: the civilization/culture centered in Europe and North America.

7. Latin American: The Catholic culture of Central and South American countries with a history of authoritarian rule.

8. Africa: multiple African cultures that are increasingly gaining assertiveness.

Huntington identified the Buddhist areas of Bhutan, Cambodia, Laos, Mongolia, Myanmar, Sri Lanka, and Thailand as separate areas from other civilizations, but maintained that these areas do not constitute a major civilization.

According to Huntington's thesis, new patterns of conflict will occur along the boundaries of different world cultures. He particularly anticipated a coalition of Islamic and Chinese cultures to work against the West as their common enemy. According to Huntington, there is historical ground for a conflict between Islamic and Christian cultures that has been aggravated in the recent times.

Both Islamic and Christian religions pursue an expansionist agenda and may see each other as the potential rivals. The West's attempt to universalize its cultural values and institutions that are deeply rooted in the Christianity and Enlightenment may collide with the Islamic traditional values. The increased communication and contact between Islam and the West has inflated the perceived differences between the two civilizations. Furthermore, without the common threat of communism, the West and Islam increasingly perceive each other as enemies. The recent revival of Islam has given Muslims a reassertion of the relevance of Islam compared to other religions. In the past decades, the Muslim population growth has created large numbers of jobless and disgruntled youth that could become suitable recruits to Islamic causes. This may only amplify the magnitude of cultural collision between the West and Islam [23].

Temporal Acceleration

One of the main features of the modern age is temporal acceleration. Simply put, the world is turning faster than ever. German philosopher Luebbe suggests that Western societies experience the "contraction of the present" because of the accelerating rates of cultural and social innovation [25]. Acceleration is almost about everything in our life, from politics and economics, to work, love, and even leisure [24]. According to Rosa, we may identify three types of acceleration: (1) the acceleration of technological change, (2) the acceleration of social change, and (3) the acceleration of the pace of life [25]. The acceleration of technological change is the most obvious type and can be defined as the speeding up of intentional processes of transport, communication, and production. It is widely accepted that we are communicating, traveling, and processing data much faster than the previous generations. In the past 15 years, the different features of microcomputers such as processing speed, price, memory capacity, and even the number and size of pixels in digital cameras have been upgraded exponentially. According to Butters' Law, the amount of data that we can transmit using optical fiber is doubling every nine months [46]. Depending on the criteria used, computer performance has increased since manual computing by a factor between 1.7 and 76 trillion [26]. The acceleration of social change is classified as speeding up of society itself including attitudes and values, fashions and lifestyles, social relations and obligations, groups, classes, milieus, and languages. The acceleration of the pace of life involves the individuals' experience of time so they consider time as scarce, feel hurried, and experience time pressure and stress [25].

Temporal acceleration is a complex phenomenon that is caused by a combination of economic, cultural, and structural factors. Within a capitalist economy, time is perceived as a highly valuable and crucial factor of production that can be translated into economic profit or loss. An acceleration of production is more efficient, more competitive, and naturally more profitable. Therefore, the processes of production, as well as distribution, and consumption constantly accelerate to create more competitive products and services. The dominant cultural ideals of modernity are associated with social change. That is why the modern Western cultures have a natural tendency to destroy the tradition and embrace novelty. The modern cultures love change for the sake of change. They define the good life as a fulfilled life that is rich in experiences and developed capacities. A fulfilled life can be attained only by doing more, by seeing more, by enjoying more, by tasting more, by being more, and by living more. Living more is possible mainly by accelerating the pace of life, having more options, and overcoming the scarcity of time. In addition to the economic and the cultural factors, the high levels of complexity of modern societies generate a higher number of options and relations whose processes require temporal acceleration. The typical family structure in a traditional society was very stable over time with generational turnover leaving the basic structure unchanged. In classical modernity, this structure was built to last for just a generation: it was organized around a couple and tended to disperse with the death of the couple. In late modernity, the family structure often lasts less than an individual life span as an increasing number of marriages are dissolved and the divorced couples remarry and build new families. Likewise, the life cycle of employment in traditional societies tended to last over many generations as the children inherited the father's profession. In classical modernity, the life cycle of employment got shorter and lasted for a life span as the children were supposed to choose their own occupations. In the postmodern societies, the life cycle of employment has become even shorter as the typical workers can change their employment multiple times during their professional lives. The effects of temporal acceleration can be seen on the product life-cycle curves in electronics as they are becoming progressively steeper and shorter in the past two decades. Indeed, the average life span of a computer has shrunk from four or five years to two years in the past decade. The short and steep product life-cycle curves are indicative of the effects of temporal acceleration on production, purchase, and consumption of many products, particularly electronic devices. First, temporal acceleration pushes the producers to create more innovative and performing devices because there is only a narrow opportunity to earn profits on a new product before the competition catches up. Then, temporal acceleration pushes the consumers to rush and buy the latest devices to fulfill their lives by buying and doing faster. That is why a large proportion of sales in electronic devices happen soon after the introduction of the product. Finally, temporal acceleration destroys stability by making the electronic devices obsolete shortly after their introduction.

Short-Termism and Myopic Management

According to Sennett, short-termism is one of the main characteristics of the contemporary culture [27]. The need for prompt responses caused by powerful communication technologies means that the future progressively shortens and ultimately melts into an extended present [28]. In other words, the limits of the future move increasingly closer to the present. Long-term strategic planning is replaced by quick and temporary fixes. High-speed, short-termism and the imperative for an immediate response characterize our contemporary culture [29]. We are living in a world where the old work ethic based on the deferred gratification, self-discipline, and long-term planning is giving way to myopia, simultaneity, and casino capitalism. Economic organizations are focusing solely on quarterly and short-term profits and are moving away from what once constituted the foundation of capitalism. We are witnessing a growing inclination toward short-term relationships in work and organization, including employment discontinuities and unstable cooperative relationships [30]. As a result, there is a shift from the Fordist mode of capitalist production to faster, more flexible, and globally coordinated economic paradigms and techniques such as just-in-time production, outsourcing, and financial globalization.

Short-termism is a pervasive cultural phenomenon whose manifestations can be found in a wide range of areas from investment, capital markets, organizational planning, strategic management, marketing, product life cycle, innovation, technology, trade, and political decision making, to more personal matters such as conjugal relations. Thanks to powerful computers and programmed algorithms, high-frequency traders whose time horizons are normally limited to fractions of a second conduct the majority of trades in financial markets. It has been suggested that the financial crisis of 2007 through 2009 was caused, at least partly, by short-termism because the market participants including mortgage originators, credit default-swap sellers, rating agencies, and investors focused only on short-term profits and neglected the markets' fundamentals. The financial markets were misled by short-term gains but, when the fundamentals emerged, house prices declined, subprime mortgages defaulted, short-term credit markets froze up, and ultimately the bubble collapsed [31]. Short-termism is an important cause of the insecurity of financial institutions [32]. Sennett (2007) argues that, by encouraging the opportunistic quest of interests, a short-term perspective may ruin trust-based mechanisms and social relationships [33]. Short-term results, often expressed as quarterly statements, could deceive managers and shareholders by hiding the essential realities of organizations. Short-termism may push managers to inflate the quarterly results and cause some early gains in the form of higher current income and stock price, but it ultimately leads to underperformance and failure. Furthermore, short-termism may encourage managers to commit unethical and even illegal behavior to reach their short-term milestones [34].

Transformation of Cultural Values

The contemporary world is experiencing significant changes in cultural values. The unprecedented economic growth in the western countries, after the Second World War and more recently in the emerging countries, is generating systematic changes in cultural values. According to modernization theory, cultural values are shaped mainly by socioeconomic conditions and a dearth or an abundance of resources [20]. As societies attain economic development and higher standards of living, they move from traditional to modern cultural values. Traditional societies emphasize the importance of parent and child ties in traditional families, deference to authority, and absolute moral standards. Furthermore, traditional societies are more likely to reject divorce, abortion, euthanasia, and suicide [20, 21]. On the other hand, modern cultures have the opposite preferences on all of these matters and are marked by secular, bureaucratic, and rational values. Interestingly, those nations with a high percentage of their workforce employed in agriculture tend to emphasize traditional values, while those with a high percentage employed in industry and service are likely to embrace modern cultural values [20, 21].

In the past four decades, due to the economic development and rising standards of living, an increasing share of the population in the Western Europe and North America has grown up taking survival for granted. As a result, the cultural values in these societies have shifted from materialism and traditional values to the postindustrial values, emphasizing subjective well-being, self-expression, and quality of life. For example, a growing number of people in the western societies are showing support for abortion, homosexuality, and same-sex marriage as they are becoming more tolerant than the previous generations used to be. The American religiousness is changing rapidly as, in one decade, the proportion of religiously unaffiliated Americans has more than doubled from 8 percent in 2003 to 22 percent in 2013 [35]. Similarly, the strong supporters of the same-sex marriage legalization have grown from 9 percent in 2003 to over 35 percent in 2013 [35]. It seems that, with some delay and imperfection, the populations of the emerging countries are following the path of cultural modernization. In China, individualist cultural values are gaining importance among the urban population whereas collectivist cultural values are in decline [36]. The differences between the cultural values of people in rich and poor societies follow a consistent pattern. Therefore, as developing countries are getting richer, they are likely to embrace the modern cultural values such as individualism, secularity and rationality, tolerance of divorce, abortion, and homosexuality (see Figure 3.3). In other words,

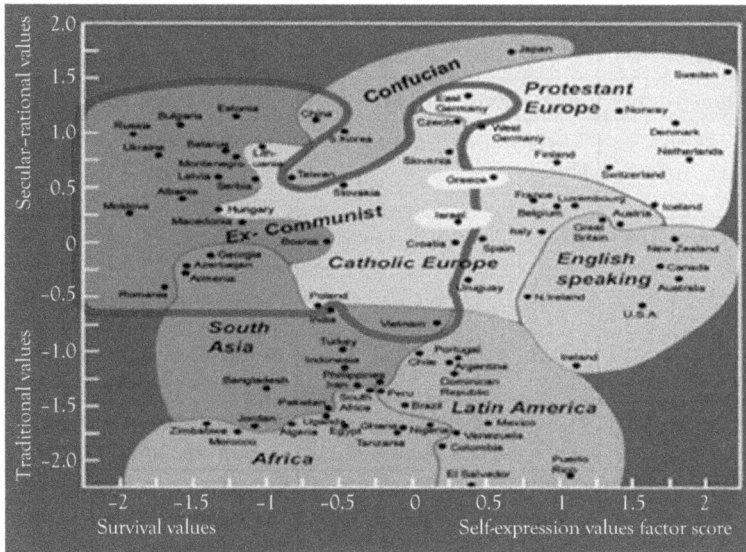

Figure 3.3 According to modernization theory, as societies attain economic development, they move from traditional to modern cultural values

economic development brings predictable and consistent changes in cultural values and pushes societies to move from traditional, religious, and survival values toward secular, rational, and self-expression values [37, 38]. It is important to bear in mind that, while economic conditions account for a considerable amount of variation in cultural values, other societal, historical, and geopolitical factors are of considerable importance.

The Culture of McDonaldization

The contemporary culture is marked by what George Ritzer labeled "McDonaldization." According to Ritzer (2008), McDonaldization is the process by which the principles of fast-food restaurants are coming to dominate multiple sectors of American society as well as of the rest of the world [39]. McDonaldization could be considered as a continuation of the Weberian bureaucracy. Ritzer argues that the success of McDonaldization can be explained through four dimensions (see Table 3.1). The first dimension is efficiency. The restaurant offers an efficient way to go from hungry to full. Workers at McDonald's also operate efficiently by

Table 3.1 The four dimensions of McDonaldization according to George Ritzer

Dimension	Explanation	Examples
1. Efficiency	The optimal method for accomplishing a task	The fastest way to get from being hungry to being full Minimization of time
2. Calculability	The quantification of objectives	Quantity is translated into quality A large amount of product delivered to the customer in a short amount of time is the same as a high-quality product.
3. Predictability	The standardization and uniformity of products and services	Always the same product, the same service, and the same task
4. Control	Influencing the customers and employees via automation	Limited menu, limited choice, and limited time for customers Limited and repetitive tasks for employees

following predesigned steps of a process. The second dimension is calculability that focuses on the quantitative aspects of McDonald's products. Examples include portion size, cost, and the amount of time it takes for the customer to get the product. This is important because people in the United States now view quantity as being as important as quality. People also calculate how much time it will take for them to get to a McDonald's restaurant rather than eating at home. Predictability is the third dimension. When people go to McDonald's, they can be sure that the product is going to be the same as the previous one. The fourth dimension of McDonaldization is control. This is exerted over the customers with the use of lines, limited menus, and uncomfortable seats. These methods of control cause people to eat quickly and leave.

Although the fast-food industry did not create the desire for efficiency in society, it helped efficiency turn into a universal reality. The streamlined process of McDonaldization has spread to other restaurants within the fast-food industry. The frozen food industry sprang up as a result of the demand to speed up and simplify home cooking. Some other areas of society that have been affected by McDonaldization include shopping, higher education, health care, and entertainment. The department stores, shopping malls, and even gas stations have all become streamlined stores allowing consumers to buy products quickly and efficiently. In the education system, universities give tests that can be graded by a machine, leaving the professors more time dedicated to research and publication. Now even more efficient modes of entertainment are available as Netflix and Amazon.com allow consumers to have movies delivered directly to their homes. People can also now listen to audio books instead of taking the time to read them.

A McDonaldized society like the United States emphasizes quantity over quality. The emphasis on quantity in the fast-food restaurants leads to the lower levels of quality, but customers are not the only people suffering from the restaurants striving for quantity instead of quality. The most efficient way to produce mass quantities of food is to have the food preparation process broken down into several individual parts. Like Henry Ford's assembly line, each worker is conducting one small task repetitively leading to their alienation and feeling no sense of personal meaning or pride in their work. In a McDonaldized society, everything must be quantifiable. For example, in the current educational system in the United States "the focus seems to be on how many students ('products') can be herded through the system and what grades they earn rather than the quality of 'what' and 'how' they learn [39]." The entire educational system has become quantified in the sense that the students are now evaluated by their grade point average (GPA) and how their GPA ranks against that of their fellow classmates. Similarly, colleges, hospitals, businesses, libraries, municipalities, and other organizations have become quantified by how they rank against their counterparts. Other products and services like books, magazines, movies, and television shows are constantly reviewed, rated, and ranked. When customers walk into a McDonald's anywhere in the world, they will get the same experience regardless of location. The employees will be wearing the same uniforms and addressing the customer with the same basic responses. The same repetitive tasks not only increase efficiency but also enable companies to produce the same products consistently each time, thus making the employee's duties predictable. Predictability has spread to other sectors and industries including entertainment, retail, transport and aviation, automotive, medicine, and education. The textbooks, curricula, and college degree programs are becoming increasingly standardized and predictable across the world. It does not matter whether you do your MBA in the United States, in Romania, or in Singapore.

In a McDonaldized culture, the nonhuman technology controls both employees and customers. For instance, customers face a variety of structural constraints and follow the norms when they enter a fast-food restaurant. The effects of nonhuman technology can be seen in universities, hospitals, and supermarkets. Fast-food restaurants today have little preparation. Everything is precooked, wrapped, cut, and seasoned. The nonhuman technology increases the control over the employees, making sure that they are doing the right orders. In hospitals, the main doctor is not the solution anymore as he used to be. A person's doctor is just the start of a long pathway that has been previously prepared. In the aviation industry, the pilots are not piloting the plane as they used to do. Instead, the computers guide the plane between takeoff and touchdown. Due to the growing effects of nonhuman technology, the human artisanship and creativity are losing their importance and are becoming worthless. In addition to its dehumanizing effects on the society, McDonaldization may paradoxically involve some inefficiencies and irrationalities. A McDonaldized society can become inefficient when there is an excess of regulations and processes. For instance, in a McDonaldized society, customer service is becoming standardized and void of any real friendliness, thus it is becoming ineffective. By giving the priority to quantity over quality, the McDonaldization process may imply negative effects on customers and employees. A McDonaldized school offers quick and cheap programs but fails to deliver a high-quality education.

References

[1] Hassi, A., and G. Storti. 2012. "Globalisation and Culture: The Three H Scenarios." In *Globalization Approaches to Diversity*, ed. H. Cuadra-Montiel, 3–20. Rijeka, Croatia: InTech Press.

[2] Prasad, A., and P. Prasad. 2006. "Global Transitions: The Emerging New World Order and its Implications for Business and Management." *Business Renaissance Quarterly* 1, no. 3, pp. 91–113.

[3] Castells, M. 1996. *The Network Society,* 469 vols. Oxford: Blackwell.

[4] Ritzer, G., and Z. Atalay, eds. 2010. *Readings in Globalization: Key Concepts and Major Debates.* John Wiley & Sons.

[5] Jaja, J.M. 2011. "Globalization or Americanization: Implications for Sub-Saharan Africa." In K.G. Deng, Globalization-Today, Tomorrow, ed. 113–24. Sciyo, Rijeka, Croatia.

[6] Beck, U. 2000. *What is Globalization?* Cornwall, UK: MPG Books, Bodmin Ltd.

[7] Berger, P. 2002. "The Cultural Dynamics of Globalization." In *Many Globalizations: Cultural Diversity in the Contemporary World,* eds. P. Berger and S.P. Huntington, 1–16. New York: Oxford University Press.

[8] Pieterse, J.N. 1995. "Globalisation as Hybridisation." In *Global Modernities,* eds. M. Featherstone, S. Lash, and R. Robertson, 45–68. London: Sage.

[9] Tomlinson, J. 2003. "Globalization and Cultural Identity" In *The Global Transformations Reader,* eds. D. Held and A. McGrew, 2nd ed., 269–78. Cambridge, UK: Polity Press.

[10] Deng, N. 2005. "On the National Literature's Tactics in the Globalization's Language Environment." *Journal of Human Institute of Humanities, Science, and Technology* 1, pp. 39–41.

[11] MacKay, H. 2004. "The Globalisation of Culture?" In *A Globalizing World? Culture, Economics Politics,* ed. D. Held, 48–84. New York: Routledge.

[12] Burton, R.E. 2009. "Globalisation and Cultural Identity in Caribbean Society: The Jamaican Case." *Caribbean Journal of Philosophy* 1, no. 1, pp. 1–18.

[13] Cvetkovich, A., and D. Kellner. 1997. "Introduction: Thinking Global and Local." *Articulating the Global and the Local,* pp. 1–30.

[14] Pieterse, J.N. 2006. "Globalization Goes in Circles: Hybridities East-West." Retrieved from http://social-theory.eu/texts/pieterse_globalization_goes_in_circles.pdf (accessed May 28, 2008).

[15] Robertson, R. 2001. "Globalization Theory 2000+: Major Problematics." In *Handbook of Social Theory,* eds. G. Ritzer and B. Smart, 458–71. London, UK: Sage Publications.

[16] Pieterse, J.N. 1996. "Globalisation and Culture: Three Paradigms." *Economic and Political Weekly* 31, no. 23, pp. 1389–93.

[17] Appadurai, A. 1990. "Disjuncture and Difference in the Global Cultural Economy." *Public Culture* 2, no. 2, pp. 1–24.

[18] Hamelink, C. 1983. *Cultural Autonomy in Global Communications.* New York, NY: Longman.

[19] Tomlinson, J. 2003. "Globalization and Cultural Identity." *The Global Transformations Reader* 2, pp. 269–77.

[20] Inglehart, R. 1997. *Modernization and Postmodernization: Cultural, Economic, and Political Change in 43 Societies.* Princeton University Press.

[21] Inglehart, R., and C. Welzel. 2005. *Modernization, Cultural Change, and Democracy: The Human Development Sequence.* Cambridge University Press.

[22] Lieber, R.J., and R.E. Weisberg. 2002. "Globalization, Culture, and Identities in Crisis." *International Journal of Politics, Culture, and Society* 16, no. 2, pp. 273–96.

[23] Huntington, S.P. 1997. *The Clash of Civilizations and the Remaking of World Order.* Penguin Books India.

[24] James, G. 1999. *Faster: The Acceleration of Just About Everything.* New York: Pantheon.

[25] Rosa, H. 2003. "Social Acceleration: Ethical and Political Consequences of a Desynchronized High–Speed Society." *Constellations* 10, no. 1, pp. 3–33.

[26] Nordhaus, W.D. 2007. "Two Centuries of Productivity Growth in Computing." *The Journal of Economic History* 67, no. 1, pp. 128–59.

[27] Sennett, R. 2011. *The Corrosion of Character: The Personal Consequences of Work in the New Capitalism.* WW Norton & Company.

[28] Petrick, K. 2016. "Strategic Planning in the 'Empire of Speed.'" *Globalizations* 13, no. 3, pp. 345–59.

[29] Hassan, R. 2003. *The Chronoscopic Society: Globalization, Time, and Knowledge in the Network Economy,* 17 vols. Peter Lang Pub Incorporated.

[30] Brose, H.G. 2004. "An Introduction Towards a Culture of Non-Simultaneity?." *Time & Society* 13, no. 1, pp. 5–26.

[31] Dallas, L. 2012. "Short-termism, The Financial Crisis, and Corporate Governance." *J. Corp. L.* 37, p. 265.

[32] Revisiting Short-termism, supra note 12, at 42. See also Emeka Duruigbo, Tackling Shareholder Short-termism and Managerial Myopia 16, 46 (April 4, 2011) (unpublished manuscript), available at http://ssrn.com/abstract=1802840

[33] Sennett, R. 2007. *The Culture of the New Capitalism.* Yale University Press.

[34] Patelli, L. 2012. Short-termism and Behavioral Ethics. School of Accountancy Daniels College of Business University of Denver.

[35] Jones, R.P., D. Cox, and J. Navarro-Rivera. 2014. *A Shifting Landscape: A Decade of Change in American Attitudes About Same-Sex Marriage and LGBT Issues.* Public Religion Research Institute.

[36] Zeng, R., and P.M. Greenfield. 2015. "Cultural Evolution Over the Last 40 Years in China: Using the Google Ngram Viewer to Study Implications of Social and Political Change for Cultural Values." *International Journal of Psychology* 50, no. 1, pp. 47–55.

[37] Inglehart, R., and W.E. Baker. 2000. "Modernization, Cultural Change, and the Persistence of Traditional Values." *American Sociological Review*, pp. 19–51.

[38] Welzel, C., R. Inglehart, and H.D. Kligemann. 2003. "The Theory of Human Development: A Cross-Cultural Analysis." *European Journal of Political Research* 42, no. 3, pp. 341–79.

[39] Ritzer, G. 2008. *The McDonaldization of Society 5*. Pine Forge Press.

[40] A snapshot of Toronto: 51% of residents were born outside Canada, Vital Signs Report finds. http://news.nationalpost.com/toronto/a-snapshot-of-toronto-51-of-residents-were-born-outside-canada-vital-signs-report-finds

[41] ACS Demographic and Housing Estimates—2009–2013 American Community Survey 5-Year Estimates. *United States Census Bureau*. Retrieved May 8, 2015.

[42] Cesari, J. November 2005. "Ethnicity, Islam, and Les Banlieues: Confusing the Issues." *Social Science Research Council* 30.

[43] Canet, R., L. Pech, M. Stewart. November 2008. "France's Burning Issue: Understanding the Urban Riots of November 2005." SSRN 1303514 Freely accessible.

[44] London disturbances - Sunday 7 August 2011. https://theguardian.com/uk/blog/2011/aug/07/tottenham-riots-police-duggan-live

[45] "School Segregation, the Continuing Tragedy of Ferguson." *ProPublica*. Retrieved November 25, 2015.

[46] Robinson, G. 2000. "Speeding Net Traffic with Tiny Mirrors." *EE Times*. Retrieved August 22, 2011.

[47] Giddens, A. 2000. *Runaway World: How Globalization is Reshaping Our Lives*. New York: Routledge.

[48] Tomlinson, J. 1999. *Globalization and Culture*. Chicago: University of Chicago Press.

[49] Conversi, D. 2002. *Walker Connor and the Study of Nationalism*. London: Routledge.

[50] Grant, N. 1997. "Democracy and Cultural Pluralism: Towards the 21st Century." In *Cultural Democracy and Ethnic Pluralism: Multicultural and Multilingual Policies in Education*, eds. R. Watts and J.J. Smolicz, 25–50. Frankfurt am Main and Berlin: Peter Lang.

[51] Skutnabb-Kangas, T., and R. Phillipson. 1998. "Language in Human Rights." *Gazette: The International Journal for Communication Studies* 60, no. 1, pp. 27–46.

CHAPTER 4

The Changing Landscape of Global Affairs

1. A Multipolar World Order
2. What Decline? Do Not Bet Against America, Yet!
3. The European Union: An Economic Giant and a Political Dwarf
4. The Rise of Nonstate Actors
5. A Comeback of Nuclear Arsenals

A Multipolar World Order

Since the end of the Cold War, we have witnessed the formation of a new multipolar world ruled by several centers of political and economic decision making [1]. The collapse of the Soviet Union and communist regimes in the 1990s marks the end of global bipolarity that had started shortly after the Second World War. While during the Cold War the two undisputable superpowers namely the United States and the Soviet Union dominated the world arena, in the past two decades, a multipolar system has been developing where numerous nations including the European countries, Russia, China, India, Japan, and Brazil are progressively gaining importance [2]. The dynamism of the new order is shaped by the presence of numerous nonstate actors including multinational corporations, investment banks, private investors, financial markets, tech giants, and supranational and regional organizations. Because of competition among various actors on the world stage, the global governance has become more diverse and more complex [3]. In tandem with the changes in the geopolitical system, the world economy has entered a multipolar phase [4]. Globalization has resulted in the ascendance of many emerging economies that are not categorized as socially advanced and completely industrialized [5]. In terms of economic growth, many developing countries have been growing much faster than developed nations of the West in the past two decades. For instance, some emerging countries including India and China grew at or above 6 percent per year between 2005 and 2010, while the developed countries grew at 2 percent or less [6]. While the global economy is not necessarily a zero-sum game, the rise of emerging countries could be the cause of the decline in the developed economies of the West (see Figure 4.1). The effects of economic growth in emerging economies are easily noticeable. For instance, gross national income (GNI) per capita increased more than sevenfold in China between 1990 and 2008. In 1990, almost 60 percent of Chinese population lived on under $1.25 per day, but in 2005 that portion was only 16 percent [6]. Similarly, other developing countries such as Brazil, India, and South Africa have experienced significant improvements in their standards of living in the past few years. The share of global exports originated in developing and emerging countries has risen from 28 percent in 1990 to 42 percent in 2007. Likewise, the share of inward flow of global foreign direct investment (FDI) to emerging countries has increased from 18 percent in 1990 to 33 percent in 2006 [5]. The FDI flows from developing economies have rapidly increased from $12 billion in 1990 to nearly $328 billion in 2010, which is equivalent to 24.8 percent of the world FDI [7]. In the past two decades, Japan and the United States' shares of the world's FDI

Gross domestic product based on purchasing power parity share of world total (in%)

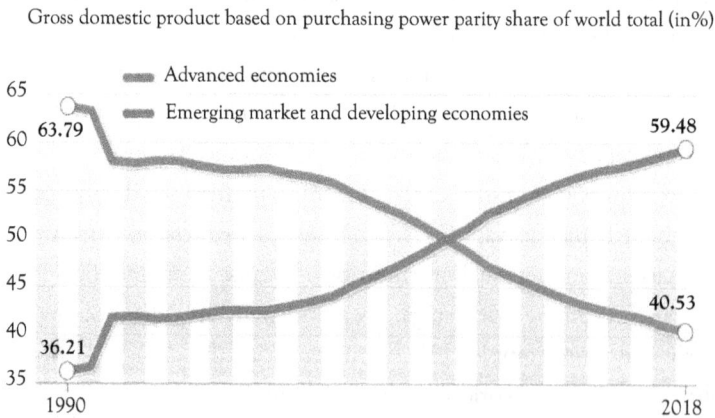

Figure 4.1 The rise of emerging countries involves a relative decline of advanced economies

Source: International Monetary Fund, World Economic Database, 2016.

have fallen while those of developing countries have risen significantly [8, 9]. Currently, the developing countries account for more than half of the global GDP, are champions of economic growth, and consume more than half of the world's energy resources. The number of emerging markets' multinationals in the Fortune Global 500 list of the world's biggest companies is going up steadily as they are expanding and acquiring new businesses across the globe at a frantic pace [10, 11, 12].

The emerging countries enjoy fairly well-developed physical and financial infrastructure but have less well-developed processes and systems of governance, regulation, and education than the world's most advanced countries [13]. As of 2016, the MSCI Emerging Markets Index included the following 21 countries: Brazil, Chile, China, Colombia, Czech Republic, Egypt, Hungary, India, Indonesia, Korea, Malaysia, Mexico, Morocco, Peru, Philippines, Poland, Russia, South Africa, Taiwan, Thailand, and Turkey (http://msci.com). According to Goldman Sachs' projections, the four largest emerging economies namely, Brazil, Russia, India, and China will overtake the economies of the group of seven largest industrialized countries (the United States, Japan, Germany, France, the UK, Italy, and Canada) by 2040 [14]. Consistent with the same projections, Brazil, Russia, India, and China along with the next 11 economies (Bangladesh, Egypt, Indonesia, Iran, South Korea, Mexico, Nigeria, Pakistan, Philippines, Turkey, and Vietnam) will be larger than the Group 7 soon after 2030.

Developing and emerging countries are capitalizing on their increased economic power to gain more influence on the global stage. In the past two decades, the Bretton Woods institutions have come under growing pressure to allow more voting power to emerging-market countries such as Brazil, India, and China [15]. The Group-20 (G-20) has replaced the Group-8 (G-8) in 2008 to include the emerging countries' influence. Similar organizational changes have occurred at the IMF [5]. Likewise, the NATO membership has been expanded to include emerging countries and a reform of the United Nations Security Council seems likely [5]. In short, emerging countries are gaining influence in many aspects of global management including environment protection, energy, health, education, pollution, climate change, migration, and security. The rise of emerging nations implies that the Western countries are facing fierce competition from numerous new players that are gradually enhancing their capabilities. For the first time since the industrial revolution, a small group of Western nations does not dominate the world economy [16]. Indeed, Europe has experienced relative political and economic decline to the benefit of Asian countries in the past 20 years. The rise of emerging countries has been described as a seismic change in the world economy, perhaps "the biggest shift since the Industrial Revolution of the 18th century" [14]. In the same vein, Zakaria (2011) suggests that we are witnessing the third great power shift in modern history. The first was the rise of the Western world, around the 15th century that made the modern world and brought about considerable revolutions in science, technology, commerce, and capitalism and ultimately the dominance of the Western world. The second shift happened in the final years of the 19th century and led to the rise of the United States as the undisputed global superpower. While in the past 20 years, America's superpower status in every realm has been largely unchallenged, there are visible indications of the rise of emerging countries, what Zakaria (2011) called "the rise of the rest." Evidently, at the military and political levels, the United States is still the unquestionable superpower, but along every other dimension including industrial, financial, social, and cultural, the distribution of power is shifting rapidly to other players mainly to emerging countries [1].

What Decline? Do Not Bet Against America, Yet!

"The rise of the rest" implies the assumption that a power shift is happening and, as a result, the United States of America is facing a drastic economic decline. This may allow others to take advantage of America's feebleness to challenge its role as the global superpower. Ordinary Americans and even many commentators and pundits have subscribed to this idea and have seen a looming American decline for a long time [17]. The so-called declinists remain cynical and view globalization and the subsequent rise of the emerging countries with a sense of apocalypse and doom. They await grave consequences for the American foreign policy and the world stability as a whole [18]. In addition to the geopolitical and economic indicators, the declinists point to many sociopolitical problems such as an inadequate education system, a weakening middle class, and a paralyzed political system in the United States to defend their pessimistic predictions about America [19]. Interestingly, the prediction of an American decline is hardly new. Since the 1960s, the commentators have been constantly forecasting dire things for the United States, every time claiming that the decline could be imminent [20, 21].

First, it seems that the commonly accepted views about China and other emerging countries rising to challenge the United States and other major Western states are based on an exaggeration of events. The facts are quite simple. The United States is and will remain the world's largest economy for a near future. The indications of American economic supremacy are abundant. Despite the rise of emerging economies, the United States has lost little of its preeminent share of world GDP over the past three decades [6]. With less than 5 percent of the world's population, America accounts for almost 23 percent of the world GDP at market exchange rates and over 19 percent at purchasing power parity (PPP) exchange rates [22]. China, with almost 20 percent of the world's population, is far behind the United States, at 9.4 percent and 13.5 percent of the world GDP at market exchange and PPP exchange rates, respectively [6]. Other emerging economies are not even considered as heavy weights in the global economy. California alone has a larger economy than Brazil and Russia. Texas' economy is nearly as big as Russia's and somewhat smaller than India's. The U.S. economy is larger than the next four largest economies altogether namely China, Japan, Germany, and the United Kingdom. Based on the standard of living, we find similar results. While standards of living are rising and poverty is declining for millions of people in emerging countries, the United States continues to be ahead by a long way. The standard of living in the United States is on average 4 times higher than that in Brazil, 6 times higher than that in China, and as much as 15 times higher than that in India. Furthermore, the United States has some incomparable advantages in size, geography, climate, energy, and natural resources that will make it an exceptional superpower. Perhaps one of the most important advantages of the United States over all other nations resides in its control over the global financial system particularly by imposing dollar as the reserve currency. As former French President Charles De Gaule rightly mentioned, using the dollar as the world reserve currency gives America an "exorbitant advantage" unlike any other. Through a dollar-based international monetary system, the United States is virtually taxing every other state, so it is able to reap more than it pays out in the provision of public goods [23].

The strength of the United States resides not only in the size of its economy but also in its astonishing competitiveness. The emerging economies like China, India, and Brazil are large but are not necessarily efficient and competitive in comparison with the United States. According to the World Economic Forum surveys, the United States has been one of the most competitive economies of the world for the past decade, while China, Russia, India, and Brazil have occupied the ranks on the bottom of the list [24]. Closely associated with competitiveness is the capacity of an economy to innovate. Innovation is perhaps the most outstanding strength of America. The United States accounted for 40 percent of total world research and development in 2008. Two-thirds of most cited researchers in science and technology are originated in the United States [24]. The United States remains the most innovative country in the world with more patents than all other countries combined. The declinists claim that the United States is sliding down the innovation list, but they cannot deny that, despite the rise of research and development in other countries, the United States still ranks among the fourth most pioneering countries of the world.

On top of all these advantages, the United States is benefiting from strong and highly competitive corporations. In 2011, 25 of the top 50 corporations were American [25]. The emerging countries' multinationals remain mainly uncompetitive and dependent on natural resources and government support. For example, a large number of corporations in China are under state control, operate within the national market, lack managerial expertise, and are deficient in terms of transparency, global branding, and sound strategic planning [26]. Another undeniable advantage of the United States resides in its military supremacy and its capacity to project power across the globe from Asia and Africa to the Middle East and Europe. The military power of other countries is not even comparable with that of the United States. While Chinese military budget has risen consistently since 1989, it is less than one-fifth of the American spending. Indeed, the United States was the world's biggest military spender in 2014, accounting for 34 percent of the global expenditure.

Another remarkable advantage of the United States resides in its capacity to build and lead wide alliance systems across the world.

Finally, in addition to all the economic, military, and political forces, America is enjoying a significant soft power thanks to a pluralist socio-political culture and an open system. The American education system continues to attract a large number of talented students from all over the world, even from those countries that are well known to have a critical view of the U.S. policies including China and Russia. Getting an education in an American college is believed not only to improve only the professional credentials but also to offer the much-needed analytical skills. It is interesting to note that the United States was home to 8 of the top 10, 37 of the top 50, and 58 of the top 100 world's universities in 2011 [28]. While the United States continues to act as a magnet for international students, the emerging countries, namely Brazil, Russia, China, and India, are facing tremendous difficulties to raise the standard of their educational systems [27]. One may suggest that one of the main causes of continuity in American/Western strength is the underlying cultural dynamism that started with the Greek philosophers, perfected during the Enlightenment in Europe, and prospered under the American capitalism.

The European Union: An Economic Giant and a Political Dwarf

With 28 member states, 510 million inhabitants, a GDP of $19.7 trillion [44], and a rich cultural heritage, the EU is certainly an important power on the world stage. In terms of GDP, the EU is the biggest economic power in the world. Furthermore, a long history of colonialism, diplomacy, and international trade make the EU an active member of the global community. Europe was developed over the past five centuries through industrialization and colonization, becoming the leading power in the current system of international relations. Most of the modern international organizations are originated in the Western Europe particularly in countries like Britain, France, and Germany. As such, the European countries in conjunction with the United States are benefiting from a great advantage in designing, affecting, and enforcing the international rules in the areas of security, cooperation, finance, trade, culture, sport, science, and technology. The European interests influence a large number of key international organizations including the United Nations, the Security Council, the IMF, and the World Bank. For example, two European states namely Britain and France are permanent members of the Security Council, and another two or three could serve as rotating members in any given year [29].

Since 2003, the EU has expressed its readiness to assume major global responsibilities. The EU has globally been recognized as a civil power standing for peace, development, human rights, and multilateralism across the world. The EU has played a benevolent role in troubled zones such as peace process in the Middle East, the Iranian nuclear deal, and the climate change accord. As such, it is possible to contrast the EU's influence with the unilateral and militaristic approach of the United States to international affairs. Consequently, in many parts of the world, the EU enjoys a high level of trust that could serve as a foundation for an effective multilateralism [30]. Nevertheless, due to its military limitations, the EU has often made only partial contributions to the stability and security of the international system (NNN-12). When comparing the EU with the United States, China, Russia, and other world powers, we need to keep in mind that the EU is by nature a different entity that relies mainly on its diplomatic approaches and soft power. The EU is an ongoing, avantgarde, and utopian project relying on multilateralism, cooperation, and peace. For that reason, the EU has been often characterized as "economic giant and political dwarf" [30].

Apparently, the EU is suffering from multiple weaknesses and challenges that limit its influence in the global affairs. A very pressing challenge is about the single currency crisis and the associated fiscal problems that have hurt the EU's credibility around the world [31]. The single currency has made the EU model less attractive not only to the member states but also to a large number of the EU citizens. As the European Council on Foreign Relations noted, "the continent seems to be losing its agency: where it was once seen as a critical part of the solution to international problems, it has now become a problem to be dealt with by others" [32]. Furthermore, the EU is suffering from a lack of coherent and independent security and defense strategy. While the member states such as France have their own national defense programs, the EU as a whole is not equipped with an effective apparatus to project hard power across the world or to defend its own security. Furthermore, the EU is still short of implementing a common foreign policy vis-a-vis global and geopolitical upheavals. The war in Iraq in 2003 showed that significant disagreements exist among the EU nation-states such as France, Germany, Italy, and Spain. If the EU can reach a higher level of political and economic integration, it will be able to overcome these challenges and express a united voice with respect to global crises. Otherwise, it is possible to predict that the EU's influence on the world stage will decline as the emerging powers, particularly Russia and Asian countries will gain economic and political weight. With the rise of emerging countries, there is an expectation for a more equitable distribution of power across the world to the detriment of the European countries that are overpresented in many international organizations from the United Nations and the Security Council to the IMF [31].

The Rise of Nonstate Actors

The Treaty of Westphalia in 1648 created the modern world order based on the principle of state sovereignty. It implied that each nation-state has sovereignty over its territory and domestic affairs, to the exclusion of all external powers, on the principle of noninterference in another country's domestic affairs. After the cold war and toward the end of the 20th century, the principle of state sovereignty has come under a growing pressure. Globalization, the new telecommunication technologies, and the integration of national economies have increased the involvement and importance of nonstate actors in international relations. The current landscape of global affairs is marked by the emergence of nonstate actors in addition to national governments. Nonstate actors are non-sovereign entities that exercise significant economic, political, or social power and influence at the national and international levels [33]. Nonstate actors may include a wide range of entities such as international organizations, multinational corporations, scientific experts, civil society groups, networks, partnerships, private military and security companies, and even transnational criminal and drug-trafficking networks [34, 35, 36, 37].

The rise of nonstate actors has contributed to a growing fragmentation of the global governance system [38]. As a consequence, we are gradually witnessing a power transfer from nation-states to nonstate actors. Nation-states and nonstate actors are both collaborating and competing on many global issues. The large corporations benefit from colossal business volumes, advanced technologies, and rare resources that enable them to have greater margins for maneuver and adaptability. The number of multinational corporations has risen from an estimated 7,000 in 1972 to some 82,000 in 2008 [39, 40]. Likewise, nongovernmental organizations (NGOs) are private, self-governing, voluntary, nonprofit, and task- or interest-oriented advocacy organizations that are increasing in number and importance [41]. As of 2008, more than 3,000 NGOs were registered as consultative groups with the United Nations Economic and Social Council [39]. Due to their flexibility, some NGOs may outcompete narrow-minded national governments. Indeed, in areas such as business, civil society, and science, nonstate actors already play a more important role than national governments do [39]. The super-rich and dominant individuals are other nonstate actors that rely on their immense wealth or power to exert their influence on the global affairs. They might include prominent industrialists, financiers, media moguls, celebrity activists, and religious leaders. These individuals often wield their influence through lobbyist groups, NGOs, multinational corporations, charity foundations, and other categories of for- or nonprofit organizations [41]. In the past two decades, the criminal and terrorist organizations have become important players on the global stage. Some nonstate violent groups such as the Lebanese Hezbollah are well positioned to exert a huge influence and even overshadow the national governments, as they constitute a better representation of the population [42]. Violent organizations might have close connections to their communities and better support them by offering public goods, especially in war-torn regions.

A Comeback of Nuclear Arsenals

Currently, there are more than 16,000 nuclear weapons in nine countries including the United States (7,200), Russia (7,500), France (300), China (260), the United Kingdom (215), Pakistan (130), India (120), Israel (80), and North Korea (10) [43]. Each of these weapons could lead to loss of thousands of lives, catastrophic levels of destruction, and long-term and lasting radioactive contamination. Due to their massive destructive capacity, the nuclear warheads are supposed to safeguard their owners against potential aggressions. Ironically, the nuclear weapons themselves might become a cause of war, conflict, and aggression [43]. In 1970, the five nuclear states namely the United States, the United Kingdom, France, China, and Russia introduced the Nuclear Nonproliferation Treaty to prevent the spread of nuclear weapons and to promote cooperation in the peaceful uses of nuclear energy [45, 46]. Furthermore, in order to enhance the nuclear stability, the nuclear states agreed upon some limitations on heavy intercontinental nuclear missiles and warheads. Thanks to these measures and the constant negotiations between the United States and the Soviet Union during the cold war, the international relations experienced some level of stability and humanity avoided the risk of a full-fledged nuclear conflict. Despite the introduction of the Nuclear Nonproliferation Treaty, other countries including India, Pakistan, and Israel continued on their nuclear programs and acquired nuclear weapons between 1970 and 1998. More recently, North Korea performed its first nuclear test in 2006 and joined the club of nuclear states [43].

The United States has an undisputable military superiority at the conventional level over all other rivals; therefore, it is considering the nuclear weapons less important. By contrast, for smaller military powers such as Russia, India, China, and Pakistan the importance of nuclear arsenals is growing because their security relies mainly on the nuclear deterrence.

China as a major Asian power is reluctant to negotiate any restriction on its nuclear arsenal. In addition to rivalry with India, China is particularly concerned about the U.S. military presence in Asia. In the recent years, the U.S.-Indian rapprochement and the American technical support of Indian nuclear program have become a source of concern for China. That is why China is in the process of modernizing its nuclear arsenal to acquire a more robust nuclear second-strike capability [43]. India and Pakistan that have joined the club of nuclear nations more recently are in political conflict and rely on their nuclear arsenal to promote their geopolitical agenda. India is committed to keep and modernize its nuclear arsenal because it faces a powerful rival as China in the East and an archenemy like Pakistan on the West. Pakistan has one of the fastest-growing nuclear arsenals as it is in a race with its archrival

India. Pakistan is capable of producing about 20 nuclear warheads a year. Considering the political instability of the country and the presence of multiple terrorist groups, the nuclear arsenal of Pakistan is a source of serious concern for the entire world. Furthermore, Pakistan reserves the right to first use of nuclear weapons in the case of an Indian conventional attack. Likewise, Israel as a small country is relying on a suspected nuclear arsenal to politically deal with its hostile neighbors and push forward its geopolitical interests. The last member of the nuclear club, North Korea has good reasons to expand its nuclear arsenal to overcome the geopolitical pressure coming from the United States and its Asian allies namely Japan and South Korea. In the case of any conflict or friction, Japan and South Korea would be able to develop nuclear weapons within a short timeframe as they already have advanced civilian nuclear infrastructure.

Russia has the largest nuclear arsenal with an estimated 7,500 warheads and boasts of its nuclear capability as a competitive advantage both politically and militarily. Considering the relative weakness of Russians at the conventional level, nuclear weapons are the source of superpower standing for Russian leaders. While the United States considers little use for nuclear weapons, Russia continues to view nuclear arms as advantageous even in ordinary military conflicts [47]. According to the *Financial Times*, in a bellicose gesture, Russia moved nuclear-capable Iskander missiles into Kaliningrad between Lithuania and Poland in 2016, warning that an impudent behavior by America may involve nuclear dimensions [48]. Similarly, in 2017, a member of Russia's parliament has declared that Russia would use nuclear weapons in any conflict in which the United States or the NATO forces entered eastern Ukraine and Crimea [49].

Based on these indications we can observe that the significance of nuclear weapons in international relations is rising again. The nuclear capacities are defining the power relationships between the United States/ NATO and Russia. In Asia, the relations between India and China on the one hand, and India and Pakistan on the other hand, are highly affected by their respective nuclear readiness. North Korea as a rogue state is relying on its nuclear capacity to defend its communist ideology. In the Middle East, Israel is relying on its nuclear arsenal not only to guarantee its security but also to gain a competitive advantage over its neighbors. Iran that has been suffering from many decades of isolation is giving up on part of its advanced nuclear program to gain economic benefits. Both the United States and Russia are modernizing their nuclear forces to enhance the accuracy and the power of their warheads. More recently, even countries such as Japan and South Korea are thinking about acquiring nuclear weapons on their own. Unfortunately, the increasing importance of nuclear power in international relations is not matched by effective efforts to control the nuclear race. The nuclear powers are not showing any serious willingness to manage the dangers of the nuclear weapons. The United States and Russia, the two largest nuclear powers, are explicitly accusing each other of having violated the previous nuclear agreements. Therefore, one may suggest that the reliance on nuclear arsenals is becoming an evident reality weighing on the global affairs.

References

[1] Zakaria, F. 2011. *The Post-American World: Release 2.0 (International Edition)*. New York, NY: W.W Norton and Company.

[2] Schweller, R.L., and X. Pu. 2011. "After Unipolarity: China's Visions of International Order in an Era of US Decline." *International Security* 36, no. 1, pp. 41–72.

[3] Chan, G. 2013. "The Rise of Multipolarity, the Reshaping of Order: China in a Brave New World?+." *International Journal of China Studies* 4, no. 1, p. 1.

[4] Zoellick, R. 2010. "The End of the Third World?" Address Delivered Before the Woodrow Wilson Center for International Scholars, Washington, DC, April 14.

[5] Berliner, J. 2010. The Rise of the Rest: How New Economic Powers are Reshaping the Globe, The Second in a Series of White Papers on the American Economy in a New Era of Globalization. NDN.com

[6] Zoellick, R. 2010. "The End of the Third World?" Address Delivered Before the Woodrow Wilson Center for International Scholars, Washington, DC, April 14.

[7] Dohse, D., R. Hassink, and C. Klaerding. 2012. "Emerging Multinationals, International Knowledge Flows and Economic Geography: A Research Agenda." Kiel Working Paper, No.1776.

[8] Kothari, T., M. Kotabe, and P. Murphy. 2013. "Rules of the Game for Emerging Market Multinational Companies from China and India." *Journal of International Management* 19, no. 3, pp. 276–99.

[9] Ramamurti, R. 2012. "Competing with Emerging Market Multinationals." *Business Horizons* 55, no. 3, pp. 241–49.

[10] Kumaraswamy, A., R. Mudambi, H. Saranga, and A. Tripathy. 2012. "Catch-Up Strategies in the Indian Auto Components Industry: Domestic Firms' Responses to Market Liberalization." *Journal of International Business Studies* 43, no. 4, pp. 368–95.

[11] Lorenzen, M., and R. Mudambi. 2012. "Clusters, Connectivity, and Catch-Up: Bollywood and Bangalore in the Global Economy." *Journal of Economic Geography* 13, no. 3, pp. 501–34.

[12] Moghaddam, K., D. Sethi, T. Weber, and J. Wu. 2014. "The Smirk of Emerging Market Firms: A Modification of the Dunning's Typology of Internationalization Motivations." *Journal of International Management* 20, pp. 359–74.

[13] Banalieva, E.R., L. Tihanyi, T.M. Devinney, and T. Pedersen. 2015. "Introduction to Part II: Emerging Economies and Multinational Enterprises." In *Emerging Economies and Multinational Enterprises (Advances in International Management)*, 28 vols, 43–69. Emerald Group Publishing Limited.

[14] Van Agtmael, A. 2007. "The Emerging Markets Century: How a New Breed of World-Class Companies is Overtaking the World." Available at SimonandSchuster.com

[15] Birdsall, N., and F. Fukuyama. 2011. "The Post-Washington Consensus-Development After the Crisis." *Foreign Affairs* 90, p. 45.

[16] Yeganeh, K.H. 2016. "An Examination of the Conditions, Characteristics, and Strategies Pertaining to the Rise of Emerging Markets Multinationals." *European Business Review* 28, no. 5, pp. 600–26.

[17] Layne, C. 2012. "This Time It's Real: The End of Unipolarity and the Pax Americana." *International Studies Quarterly* 56, no. 1, pp. 203–13.

[18] Quinn, A. 2011. "The Art of Declining Politely: Obama's Prudent Presidency and the Waning of American Power." *International Affairs* 87, no. 4, pp. 803–24.

[19] Luce, E. 2012. *Time to Start Thinking: America in the Age of Descent.* New York: Atlantic Monthly Press.

[20] Calleo, D.P. 2009. *Follies of Power: America's Unipolar Fantasy.* Cambridge University Press.

[21] Wade, R. 2013. "The Art of Power Maintenance: How Western States Keep the Lead in Global Organizations." *Challenge* 56, no. 1, pp. 5–39.

[22] Wade, R.H. 2011. "Emerging World Order? From Multipolarity to Multilateralism in the G20, the World Bank, and the IMF." *Politics & Society* 39, no. 3, pp. 347–78.

[23] Norrlof, C. 2010. *America's Global Advantage: US Hegemony and International Cooperation.* Cambridge University Press.

[24] Galama, T., and Hosek, J. 2008. *US competitiveness in science and technology.* Santa Monica, CA: Rand Corporation.

[25] Cox, M. 2012. "Power Shifts, Economic Change and the Decline of the West?" *International Relations* 26, no. 4, pp. 369–88.

[26] Shambaugh, D. April–June 2012. "Are China's Multinational Corporations Really Multinational?" In *East Asia Forum Quarterly* 4, no. 2, pp. 7–14.

[27] Luce, E. 2012. "Time to Start Thinking: America in the Age of Descent." Grove/Atlantic, Inc.

[28] QS World University Rankings—2012, available at https://topuniversities. com/university-rankings/world-university-rankings/2012

[29] Smith, K.E. 2013. "Can the European Union be a Pole in a Multipolar World?." *The International Spectator* 48, no. 2, pp. 114–26.

[30] Messner, D. 2007. The European Union: Protagonist in a Multilateral World Order or Peripheral Power in the "Asia-Pacific" Century?

[31] Smith, K.E. 2013. "Can the European Union be a Pole in a Multipolar World?." *The International Spectator* 48, no. 2, pp. 114–26.

[32] European Council on Foreign Relations, "Introduction," European Foreign Policy Scorecard 2012, 9. http://ecfr.eu/content/entry/european_foreign_policy_scorecard_2012

[33] La-Porte, M.T. 2015. The Legitimacy and Effectiveness of Non-State Actors and the Public Diplomacy Concept.

[34] Moravcsik, A. 2010. "Europe, the Second Superpower." *Current History* 109, no. 725, p. 91.

[35] Dingwerth, K., and P. Pattberg. 2006. "Global Governance as a Perspective on World Politics." *Global Governance: A Review of Multilateralism and International Organizations* 12, no. 2, pp. 185–203.

[36] Biermann, F., and P.H. Pattberg, eds. 2012. *Global Environmental Governance Reconsidered*. MIT Press.

[37] Karns, M.P., and K.A. Mingst. 2013. "International Organizations and Diplomacy." In *the Oxford Handbook of Modern Diplomacy*. Oxford, UK.

[38] Jang, J., J. McSparren, and Y. Rashchupkina. 2016. Global Governance: Present and Future.

[39] Falkner, R. 2011. "Global Governance: The Rise of Non-State Actors: A Background Report for the SOER 2010 Assessment of Global Megatrends." European Environment Agency.

[40] UNCTAD (United Nations Conference on Trade and Development). 2009. World Investment Report 2009. Retrieved February 18, 2010.

[41] Bieler, A., R. Higgott, and G. Underhill, eds. 2004. *Non-State Actors and Authority in the Global System*. Routledge.

[42] Jakobi, A.P. 2010. Non-State Violence and Political Order: A View on Long-Term Consequences of Non-State Security Governance.

[43] Strategic Trends 2016 is also electronically available at www.css.ethz.ch/publications/strategic-trends

[44] Eurostat—Population on January 1, 2016. Retrieved July 11, 2016.

[45] Treaty on the Non-Proliferation of Nuclear Weapons (NPT) https://un.org/disarmament/wmd/nuclear/npt/

[46] North Korea Nuclear Tests: What Did They Achieve? BBC News, September 3, 2017. http://bbc.com/news/world-asia-17823706

[47] Russia's Nuclear Weapons: Everything You Always Wanted To Know (But Were Afraid To Ask), Published on *The National Interest*. http://nationalinterest.org

[48] Russia: Putting the 'Nuclear Gun' Back on the Table, Retrieved from November 15, 2016, https://ft.com/content/03dfeb98-aa88-11e6-9cb3-bb8207902122

[49] Russian Lawmaker: We Would Use Nukes if US or NATO Enters Crimea. http://defenseone.com/threats/2017/05/russian-lawmaker-we-would-use-nukes-if-us-or-nato-enters-crimea/138230/

CHAPTER 5

The Rising Powers: China, Brazil, India, Russia, and South Africa

1. BRICS: The Agreement on Disagreements
2. China
3. Brazil
4. Russia
5. India
6. South Africa

BRICS: The Agreement on Disagreements

The BRICS countries consisting of Brazil, Russia, India, China, and South Africa are large and populous countries that experience fast-expanding domestic markets and benefit from the abundant and affordable workforce. While there has been some slowdown in Russia and Brazil, the BRICS have witnessed remarkable growth rates over the course of the past 15 years between 2002 and 2016. During the last decade, the BRICS countries have enhanced their legitimacy by playing important roles in the world economic system and its institutions including WTO, the Group of 20 (G-20), and the United Nations' Framework Convention on Climate Change [1]. As the top 10 largest world's economies, the BRICS have formed strong political and economic relations with the rest of their region and are gradually acting as the leaders for regional cooperation. They are protecting regional security by either working through regional institutions or coordinating with major external players [2]. China and Russia are permanent members of the United Nations' Security Council. All the BRICS members favor the United Nations to play a dominant role in international affairs including peace and security, domestic turmoil, global pandemics, terrorism, and proliferation of weapons of mass destruction [2]. Except for Russia, the BRICS countries are acting as global players for the first time in their history. They are in the process of modernizing their military forces to protect their geopolitical and strategic interests [3]. Yet, the BRICS are still facing significant social and structural shortcomings that undermine their economic and political assertiveness. For instance, all the BRICS countries are suffering from widespread corruption levels, high rates of illiteracy, weak institutions, deficient regulations, poverty and lack of sociopolitical stability, economic inequalities, overreliance on commodities exports, and a dependence on foreign direct investments [4].

In order to enhance their foreign interests, the BRICS are translating their economic strength into political influence on the world stage (see Figure 5.1). The BRICS club has become a platform for dialogue and cooperation in economic, financial, and political domains [2]. Relying on their increasing influence, the BRICS would speak on behalf of emerging countries in the international settings, promoting a more reasonable, representative, and balanced international order. While BRICS do not necessarily challenge the present international system, they tend to seek an alternative world order. In the past decade, and especially after the financial crisis of 2008, the BRICS members have cooperated to launch reforms in the global financial institutions in order to make them more

Figure 5.1 The BRICS countries aim at playing a more important role on the world stage

representative, open, inclusive, and transparent. In the past five years, four important members namely Brazil, South Africa, India, and China have been working together on international negotiations about climate change. Consistent with these goals and policies, the members have recently tried to reinforce their cooperation within the BRICS organization. At the fifth BRICS Summit in 2013, the member countries declared the formation of a new development bank to mobilize resources from the BRICS nations for sustainable development in developing countries [4]. With regard to foreign affairs, the BRICS states have pronounced their concerns about the global supremacy of the United States and its use of military power around the world. For that reason, they have opposed the U.S. war in Iraq and expressed their own opinions with regard to crises such as nuclear issues in North Korea and Iran [4]. The BRICS countries have occasionally opposed the traditional Western powers on many global issues. For instance, Russia and China have long been fighting against the Western hegemony within the Security Council. Similarly, Brazil has been confronting the United States on the Free Trade Area of the America. The common goal of opposing the Western powers may be a reason to create more unity among the BRICS members [5]. The BRICS countries have many commonalities with regard to multipolarity and antipathy against the American hegemony, but these shared interests do not seem strong enough to form a coherent and influential institution [6]. The BRICS organization remains a fragile community due to the high level of disparity among the state members and their diverging interests and priorities.

Furthermore, the BRICS nations have dissimilar economic structures (Table 5.1). Brazil has a competitive agricultural sector, Russia depends on its vast oil and gas resources, and India is gaining competitiveness in information technology and service sector, whereas China relies mainly on its competitive manufacturing [7]. In terms of economic and military power, China is far ahead of South Africa, Brazil, and India. While Russia is still relying on the Soviet military capabilities, it is lagging behind China and India in economic growth [5]. The Sino-Russian and Sino-Indian relationships have been historically problematic and are easy to turn poisonous again. Russia might be uncomfortable with the ascending position of China suggesting that China could eventually pose a great threat to

Table 5.1 *The club of BRICS represents countries with dissimilar socioeconomic fundamentals*

	Population (2016)	Land area (sq. mi.)	GDP (2016) (US$)	GDP per capita (2016) (US$)	Literacy (%)	GDP growth rate (2016) (%)
China	1.379 billion	3.705 million	11.2 trillion	8,123.18	93	6.7
India	1.324 billion	1.269 million	2.264 trillion	1,709.39	61	7
Brazil	207.7 million	3.288 million	1.796 trillion	8,649.95	90.3	–3.6
Russia	144.3 million	6.602 million	1.283 trillion	8,748.36	99.4	–0.2
South Africa	55.91 million	470,900	294.8 billion	5,273.59	86.4	0.3

Source: World Bank Data.

Russia's security. Likewise, there is competition between China and India over their influence in neighboring countries such as Cambodia, Nepal, and Myanmar. Due to the high levels of rivalry, China and Russia are not favorable to the ascendance of India to the United Nations' Security Council seat [4]. The divergences over the military dimension of BRICS are even more noticeable. Russia is the only state member interested in forming a BRICS military and defense alliance in order to counterbalance the American and the North Atlantic Treaty Organization (NATO)'s influence. While China is ambivalent about the formation of a BRICS military alliance, other members particularly India and Brazil remain reluctant toward such an initiative as they seek better relations with the United States [4]. The BRICS members may reach some agreements on cooperation in areas like information exchange, but they are not likely to reach a full-fledged and comprehensive military alliance in near future. With regard to trade policies, the BRICS members have stayed at odds and have not been able to develop a harmonized strategy at the WTO. For instance, Brazil and South Africa tend to take a more aggressive attitude in favor of trade liberalization for agricultural products, whereas India and China pursue the protection of their agricultural sectors [4]. The relations between Russia, China, and India are marked by distrust and rivalry as they severely compete over geopolitical influence and resources in Asia [8]. Furthermore, the BRICS countries have significant cultural and ideological differences that might hinder their close cooperation on the global affairs. For instance, China relies on a communist totalitarian political system in conjunction with a state-capitalism model. By contrast, Brazil, South Africa, and India are the pluralistic but deficient democracies that face many internal problems due to poverty, corruption, and illiteracy. Russia seems like a formal democracy, but indeed it relies on an authoritarian oligarchy curbing freedom of speech and other civil liberties [4]. Another major issue with the BRICS is whether to accept new members or limit the membership to the existing level. This matter might have major implications for the future of BRICS, as many countries from the so-called N11 nations (The Next 11: Bangladesh, Egypt, Indonesia, Iran, South Korea, Mexico, Nigeria, Pakistan, the Philippines, Turkey, and Vietnam) have been considered as candidates [9].

The United States and the Western powers may exploit the differences among the BRIC member states to divide them and continue their dominance on the global stage. For instance, the United States may capitalize on the Sino-Indian rivalry to counter the hegemony of China and the BRICS as a whole. While Russia is an assertive and even aggressive power, other BRICS members such as Brazil and South Africa will be probably satisfied with some slight changes in the regional or global governance systems. Even if these changes materialize, the structure of global governance will still be under the control of the United States and the North Atlantic Alliance. Considering their massive demographic powers, China and India will not limit their requests to some reforms of the global governance. After all, China and India represent more than 40 percent of the world's population and naturally they will pursue loftier aspirations and radical transformations. The ambitions of these two Asian giants and the subsequent transformations may involve fiction or conflict with the old Western powers, particularly with the United States. If the declining Western powers do not accept the new realities, the transformation of the global governance could lead to violence and military confrontation [6].

China

By developing its manufacturing industries, China has been pursuing an active export strategy to fuel an astonishing economic growth averaging 10 percent a year during the past three decades. Because of this massive economic growth, China has lifted more than 800 million people out of poverty. Yet, China is facing multiple challenges that could jeopardize its very stability. Politically, China faces many internal concerns including unrest in the west of the country and the dispute over Taiwan and Tibet. In the Western Xinjiang province, China has difficult relations with its Muslim minorities. The most important challenge is about the viability of the China's authoritarian one-party political system that has become a strange combination of communist political system and state-owned capitalism. There is some speculation that eventually the economic reforms and the ensuing growth and development will require a drastic change in the Chinese political system. The Chinese economic model itself may be unviable in future. For the past three decades, China has powered its economy by relying on a manufacturing industry, which has benefited mainly from the cheap and abundant workforce. This model of economic growth could be less practical in the long term as the country is already witnessing higher wages, shrinking workforce, and improving working conditions that ultimately will reduce its manufacturing competitiveness. Furthermore, the Chinese manufacturing model is dependent on the consumption of huge amounts of fossil fuel and lenient environmental standards that will not be sustainable in the long run [7]. Substantial socioeconomic changes are essential in order for China's growth to be sustainable. Indeed, transitioning from middle-income to high-income levels is generally more challenging than moving up from low to middle income. The sustainability of growth is a top priority and, for that reason, China has started to modernize its economy by allocating more funding to research and development. The modernization of education system and labor force implies that China may boost its economic growth by relying on knowledge-based sectors instead of cheap labor manufacturing. Chinese economic growth is likely to be affected significantly by the demographic trends. As a result of China's one-child policy that was introduced in 1977, a large portion of the population will grow old together, putting a great pressure on many segments including the labor market, pension plans, education, and health care services. As China is moving away from the cheap labor manufacturing, the negative effects of population shrinking may be mitigated by automation [10].

The French military and political mastermind Napoléon Bonaparte famously once said: let China sleep, for when China wakes she will shake the World. One of the most important facts in the contemporary world is that China is waking up. China has already the second largest economy, the third biggest land area, and the world's largest population. China's increasing economic weight combined with its geopolitical and demographic standing will have substantial effects on all aspects of global governance in the next decades. China is still reluctant to behave assertively to assume its role as a global leader, but in reality, China is a global hegemon. China's enormous currency reserves make China an incontestable leader in the international financial markets. Chinese domestic policies on monetary and fiscal matters inevitably shake the global financial markets [11].

The transition of China from a poor, undeveloped, and agrarian society to a world power may pose serious threats to the old Western hegemony in the international system. On the one hand, China is overtly challenging the American influence in the Asia-Pacific region [12]. On the other hand, China has been encouraging regional cooperation processes that do not include the United States. For example, the Shanghai Cooperation Organization made up of China, Russia, Uzbekistan, Kyrgyzstan, Kazakhstan, and Tajikistan has become a platform for Chinese influence [13]. The Shanghai Cooperation Organization's goals in international affairs are principally the same goals found in the foreign policy directives of China [14]. Likewise, China is raising its involvement in ASEAN to gain regional influence [15]. In the past few years, China has been developing strategies toward resource and energy-rich countries in Africa, Asia, and Latin America. By challenging the American and Western hegemony, China has been developing some privileged economic and political relations with countries like Burma, Sudan, Zimbabwe, and Iran. Similarly, China has become Africa's single largest trading partner as Chinese businesses have established a significant presence in Africa by building infrastructure and running mines and oil fields [16].

Despite its lofty aspirations, China's top priority is modernization and economic development. To this end, as early as 1978, China has adopted a practical approach and has reduced the role of communist ideology in economic policy. The main argument behind this strategy is that social and political stability will follow the economic development and, as long as economic growth continues, the political system will remain stable and strong. Indeed, pragmatism is one of the main features of China in dealing with both domestic and international challenges. In the words of the late Deng Xiaoping, it does not matter whether a cat is white or black, as long as it catches mice [17]. Not surprisingly, China has kept its communist political system, while it has emerged as the world's fastest-growing economy for over three decades. The Chinese foreign policy is marked by a sense of realism to promote the country's economic interests. Consistent with this pragmatic approach, China has based foreign policy on peaceful development on the one hand, and international engagement on the other hand [18]. China is emphasizing that its economic development and military expansion do not represent a threat to other countries.

China, at least for now, is not seeking tensions with other powers, particularly with the United States. As the Chinese legendary General Sun Tzu mentioned, the supreme art of war is to subdue the enemy without fighting.

Brazil

After the political turmoil in the 1980s and the subsequent economic crises, Brazil finally arose as a stable and democratic country. Since then, Brazil has become an important player in Latin America and an emerging power in global affairs. The importance of Brazil as a major global player hinges on its demographic, geographic, and economic capacities. Brazil is the largest country in Latin America and the fifth largest one in the world [19]. It is home to almost 200 million people and its GDP of $3 trillion makes it the ninth largest economy in the world in 2016 (World Bank). As a member of the BRICS, Brazil has economically underperformed in the past two decades and its performance cannot be compared to China's, India's, and even Russia's growth. For instance, between years 2000 and 2006, Brazil's GDP grew only 3 percent that underperformed not only the BRICS but also the global average [20]. Since the fall of commodity prices in 2011, the GDP growth has been consistently lower than predicted, and some fundamental weaknesses underlying the economy have reappeared, including an inefficient and complex tax system, a sizeable informal sector, poor infrastructure, corruption, limited competition, high costs of starting a business, and high tariff rates. Despite all the apparent weakness, Brazil is characterized by a quite modern economy with a significant service sector (65 percent of the GDP) and small agriculture sector (7 percent of the GDP). While Brazil enjoys a very competitive agricultural sector, the share of agriculture in its GDP is much lower than industry and service. The Brazilian economy has been struggling for the past four years mainly due to lower prices of commodities that constitute the main Brazilian exports. Brazil's economy is highly dependent on Chinese growth and its appetite for natural resources. Brazil ranks 24 among the world's largest exporters with a modest share in world total exports of 1.32 percent (U.S.$242 billion) [4]. Due to the commodities boom, Brazil has shown a trade surplus for many years during the 1980s and the 1990s, but more recently the country has run trade deficits and has put in place some protectionist policies that are likely to impede its growth. A major concern about the future of Brazilian economy is the extent that its manufacturing sector can compete with the low-priced products made in China. Because of intense competition originating from China, the Brazilian manufacturers are losing market shares both domestically and internationally [21].

By advocating multilateralism, peace, and stability, Brazil has assumed important international responsibilities in the global and regional organizations such as the Common Market of the South (Mercosur) and the Union of South American Nations (Unasur) [22]. In 2009, Brazil was one of the main founders of the South American Defense Council to enhance peace and democratic stability in the region [4]. Brazil enjoys friendly relations with most of the world countries and does not seem to have any natural enemies in South America. Consequently, the welcoming relations with the neighboring states and a tendency toward trade and economic cooperation are noticeable in the Brazilian foreign policy. The real influence of Brazil is a soft power that does not result from its military capacity but derives from cultural, economic, and diplomatic capabilities [23]. Militarily, Brazil is quite weak compared to other BRICS countries such as Russia and China. Since Brazil does not see any security threat on its borders, it does not see military modernization as a top priority and has the smallest military budget among the BRICS members [24]. Since the 1980s, Brazil has scrapped some military programs associated with the production of weapons of mass destruction and has adhered to international treaties. In the 1990s, Brazil abandoned its nuclear weapons program to create an environment for regional and global cooperation [25]. Nonetheless, Brazil is highly involved in the United Nations' peacekeeping missions across the world and more recently has increased its presence in international and regional institutions.

Brazil is keen to exert its influence on the global affairs via South–South multilateral cooperation. Brazil's role as a global player in the world political affairs is often acknowledged and accepted by the Western powers. Therefore, Brazil can delicately act as an intermediary between the developed and developing countries. Indeed, very few countries like Brazil have gained the trust of both developed and developing countries

[26]. Brazil capitalizes on its geographic and economic weight to advocate the representativeness and equity in international institutions such as the Security Council. Very similar to China, Brazil portrays an image of peacefulness on the world stage and emphasizes that its economic rise does not pose any threat to other nations, rather enhances the global peace and security.

Russia

Russia seems to have fewer commonalities with other emerging countries such as China, India, and Brazil. After the collapse of the Soviet Union in 1991, the Russian Federation abruptly replaced the communist system with new political and economic systems. The new Russian Federation had a reduced economy, was a smaller inland area, and naturally enjoyed much less power and status on the world stage. The so-called shock therapy, which included a swift abolition of the centrally planned economy, privatization, and transition to the market-based system, created too much change in a short period. In the absence of strong institutions, the "shock therapy" caused a power vacuum, economic mismanagement, and political turmoil in the early 1990s. As a result, a small number of influential oligarchs gained control over the financial resources and quickly enriched themselves to the detriment of the Russian population. In 1999, Vladimir Putin took office and implemented some strategies to stabilize the economy and strengthen the central government in Moscow. Since then, Putin has acted as the de facto Tsar of Russia and has relied on security and military elites to consolidate power [7]. Due to higher energy prices, his policies have resulted in higher economic growth in the past two decades. Among all the BRICS members, Russia's economy is dependent most heavily on the energy sector. With the largest amount of natural gas reserves and the second-largest oil reserves in the world, Russia is highly reliant on revenues generated from gas and oil exports, which represented about 20 to 25 percent of the Russian GDP in 2009 [27]. The energy sector has been driving the economic growth in Russia for the past two decades, resulting in higher income levels and the emergence of a new middle class. At the same time, the dependence on oil and gas sectors has made Russia vulnerable to the fluctuations of energy prices as happened between 2008 and 2009 and more recently between 2014 and 2016. Furthermore, the overreliance on energy sector has contributed to the lower industrial competitiveness, unaccountability, widespread corruption, and stagnation. The efforts and policies of the Russian Federation to diversify the economy have been mainly unsuccessful. Therefore, the dependence of Russia on energy sector is expected to continue, at least for near future. Since 2013, the Russian economy has been hit by multiple sanctions imposed by the United States and the EU particularly over its military intervention in Ukraine and Crimea.

As the natural successor state of the Soviet Union, Russia has inherited the privilege of a permanent seat on the UN Security Council. Relying on its vast territory, its immense natural resources, and its powerful army, Russia is keen to exert its influence on the world stage and promote its geopolitical and economic interests. Nevertheless, Russia cannot be considered as a superpower comparable to the United States or China. The Russian economy constantly underperforms and is not able to innovate. The political process is hardly transparent and the politicians are under the direct influence of oligarchs. Despite more than two decades of reform, entrepreneurship is not a driving force and the business corruption is rampant. Poor human rights, corruption, and authoritarian governance often blemish the Russian image. Unlike some other members of the BRICS, Russia cannot exert soft power to influence global affairs. Similar to the Soviet Union, the Russian Federation actively and aggressively seeks geopolitical dominance. Over the course of the past decade, Russia has resorted to numerous coercive actions and military interventions in order to protect its interests at the international or regional level. The military interventions in Chechnya, South Ossetia, Georgia, Ukraine, Crimea, and more recently Syria, the cyber-attacks on the United States, the EU, Estonia, and numerous other countries, and the oil and gas cutoffs by the partly state-owned Gazprom are some typical examples of the Russian aggressiveness on the world stage [7]. Among the BRICS countries, Russia has a proclivity to use force to achieve its strategic objectives. While economic interests play an important role in shaping the Russian foreign policy, the military strength remains central to the Russian Federation under Putin. Russia views the West and the United States in particular as its natural competitors and puts blame on them for most of its socioeconomic problems. Furthermore, Moscow is sensitive to Western expansion to the East, promotion of liberal democratic principles, and the hostile expansion of NATO to its regional sphere of influence [4]. That is why Russia is willing to capitalize on the BRICS club to promote a multipolar world and offset the American expansion. Historically, the Russian ambitions are centered on the Russian sovereignty and territorial integrity, an exacerbated nationalism, and a thirst for global influence [28]. As a consequence, the Western values such as the rule of law, democracy, freedom of speech, political pluralism, transparency, and minority rights are often sacrificed for the sake of national interest and a central authority [29]. In short, the Russian Federation strategic culture is characterized by competitiveness, political assertiveness, and a strong desire to restore the glory of the Soviet era [29]. These features make Russia very different from other BRICS members that are preoccupied primarily by economic growth and social development.

India

With a large and rapidly growing population estimated at 1.3 billion, India is poised to overtake China as the world's most populous country sometime in the next five years. After its independence in 1947 and particularly during the Cold War era, India was a leading force behind the Non-Aligned Movement and sought to offset the influence of Western powers on the world stage. In the early 1990s after many decades of economic stagnation and low growth, India chose to abandon its left-wing, inward-looking, and interventionist policies and initiated drastic reforms to liberalize the national economy [30]. Similar to China, since then India has experienced a consistent period of high economic growth averaging at 5 percent per year [30]. There is no sign of a slowdown in India and, according to the World Bank and IMF, the significant economic growth of India is expected to continue in the next few years [7]. India is already a member of the G20. While Indian economy is the same size as those of Brazil and Russia, what makes India different is its huge potential for a sustainable growth until 2020 at an annual average rate of 8 percent [7]. If Indian economy grows as expected, then it will be larger than the U.S. economy in 2050 [7]. In order to maintain future economic growth, India needs to continue reforms and improve multiple areas including education, agriculture, and infrastructure [31]. The main engine of Indian economy is service sector and particularly information technology that accounts for 35 percent of India's exports whose revenue has increased from 3.3 billion in 1998 to an enormous 87 billion in 2008. Despite this phenomenal growth, India is still a very poor country that grapples with various social problems. According to the United Nations reports, almost 33 percent of India's population lives below the one dollar a day (purchasing power parity (PPP)) poverty line and almost 70 percent lives on less than two dollars per day [4]. A poor infrastructure, high illiteracy levels, a weak currency, high inflation rates, low agricultural productivity, and a small manufacturing sector are other hurdles that constrain Indian economic growth [4]. Moreover, India often is shaken by instability, terrorism, and conflict between Hindus and Muslims and frictions with its western neighbor Pakistan over territorial disputes in the Kashmir province. The frictions between India and Pakistan stem from a wide range of religious, geopolitical, and territorial factors and are expected to aggravate as the population in both countries are growing rapidly. The Indo-Pakistani conflict is particularly frightening because the two countries possess nuclear weapons [32]. In addition to conflicts with Pakistan, India has some difficult relations with other neighboring countries, notably China, its closest rival in the BRICS club, a nuclear superpower, and a rising economy. Since its independence in 1947, India has implemented a Western-style democratic system and in the recent years has developed friendly relations with the United States. More recently, India and the United States have been cooperating on their mutual interests including the war on terrorism, democracy, and the Asian geopolitics [33]. India is one of the main supporters of change in the international governance structures, particularly in the UN Security Council. To this end, the Indian foreign policy is centered on promoting representativeness, multilateralism, and inclusiveness of the international system. Nevertheless, India maintains a pragmatic approach to international relations and abides by the international law. Complexity and high levels of unpredictability mark India's behavior on the world stage. India can be considered as a distinct civilization that actively seeks self-sufficiency, as it has no natural friends in the world. Despite its enormous population, Indian military power is still very limited and is far from exerting influence across the world. In brief, the approach of India to international relations is mainly prudent and nonconfrontational.

South Africa

With a population of 55 million and an economy of $300 billion, South Africa is the smallest member of the BRICS club. Demographically and economically, South Africa is not comparable to other nations of BRICS. Indeed, South Africa was not part of the original BRIC acronym that was coined by Goldman Sachs in 2001. There is some doubt regarding the admittance of a relatively small economy like South Africa to the club of giants [34]. The nature of the association between South Africa and other BRICS members has been subject to extensive speculation [34]. Nevertheless, the addition of South Africa to BRICS enhanced the representativeness, legitimacy, and credibility of the organization. After the end of apartheid in 1994, South Africa has acted as a stabilizing force in Africa and has shown itself as the role model for economic development in Africa. In three decades, South Africa has changed from international pariah under the apartheid to a model for democracy, economic development, and reconciliation [35]. As a young and unsettled democracy, South Africa is still redefining itself, working to strengthen its political and economic institutions and overcome its social and racial rifts. Considering the experience of South Africa with apartheid, the country can play an important role in bridging the gaps between the developing and developed countries. Accordingly, South Africa has been seeking alternatives to the current world order based on a more active participation of developing countries in the global institutions. The African Union and pan-African solidarity are the focus of South African foreign policy. Many African countries consider South Africa as a regional power that can play a central role in resolving disputes on the African continent. South Africa is keen to collaborate with the United States and the EU, as well as with the other BRICS countries on multiple regional and global matters. It has reinforced the BRICS's image as a valid representative of Africa [4].

South Africa's economic growth in the past two decades has provided the country with an opportunity to exert its influence on the world stage, but its demographic and sociocultural constraints have impeded the country from playing a more active role. South Africa benefits from strong foreign and domestic investment flows and has a solid economic presence on the African continent. The country is an important center for multinationals headquarters. It plays a pivotal role in logistics, distribution, and sourcing for regional markets [36]. Above all, South Africa benefits from strong democratic institutions, including a progressive constitution that preserves political and socioeconomic rights, and provides for checks and balances on the power of the government [37]. As an emerging economy, South Africa still is facing multiple challenges that could curb its economic growth in the next decade. Social divide, racial rift, illiteracy, and unemployment not only limit the South African progress but also pose serious threats to its stability in future. Bribery, embezzlement, and corporate fraud are shaking the country. Corruption is a widespread disease that is affecting economic development, education, and public services [33]. In the absence of a significant change, South Africa could lose its place among other emerging economies and may become a typical developing country [38, 39].

References

[1] Macfarlane, S. 2006. "The 'R' in BRICs: is Russia an Emerging Power?." *International Affairs* 82, no. 1, pp. 41–57.

[2] Haibin, N. 2012. "BRICS in Global Governance. A Progressive Force." *Friedrich Ebert Stiftung Perspective.*

[3] Darling, D. June 20, 2010. "BRIC Military Modernization and the New Global Defense Balance." *The Faster Time.*

[4] Degaut, M., and C.E. Meacham. 2015. *Do the BRICS Still Matter?.* Center for Strategic & International Studies.

[5] Shaw, T.M., A.F. Cooper, and G.T. Chin. 2009. "Emerging Powers and Africa: Implications for/from Global Governance?." *Politikon* 36, no. 1, pp. 27–44.

[6] Käkönen, J. 2015. "BRICS as a New Constellation in International Relations." *Mapping BRICS Media*, p. 25.

[7] Stefánsson, O.I.N. 2012. The BRICs and International Relations: An Assessment of the Potential Leaders in a Global Future.

[8] Trenin, D. February 2012. *True Partners? How Russia and China See Each Other.* London: Center for European Reform.

[9] Wilson, D., A. Stupnytska, T. Poddar, A. Bhundia, P. Morra, and S. Ahmed. 2007. Global Economics Paper No: 153. Goldman Sachs.

[10] Sachs, G. 2007. BRICS and Beyond. Goldman Sachs Global Economics Group.

[11] Hefeker, C., and A. Nabor. 2002. Yen or Yuan? China's Role in the Future of Asian Monetary Integration.

[12] Desker, B. 2008. "New Security Dimensions in the Asia–Pacific." *Asia Pacific Review* 15, no. 1, pp. 56–75.

[13] Gu, J., J. Humphrey, and D. Messner. 2008. "Global Governance and Developing Countries: The Implications of the Rise of China." *World Development* 36, no. 2, pp. 274–92.

[14] Harden, B.E. 2014. "The Diplomatic Ambitions of the BRIC State: Challenging the Hegemony of the West." *Journal of International Relations and Foreign Policy* 2, no. 2, pp. 1–18.

[15] "Asia's never-Closer Union." *The Economist*, February 4, 2010. http://economist.com/world/asia/displaystory.cfm?story_id=15452622 (accessed March 10, 2010).

[16] Taylor, I. 2008. "China in Africa by AldenChrisLondon: Zed Books, 2007. pp. 136,£ 12.99 (pbk.)." *The Journal of Modern African Studies* 46, no. 2, pp. 325–26.

[17] Li, H. 1977. *China's Political Situation and the Power Struggle in Peking.* Hong Kong, People's Republic of China: Lung Men Press.

[18] Johnson, K.D. 2009. *China's Strategic Culture: A Perspective for the United States.* Strategic Studies Institute.

[19] Harden, B.E. 2014. "The Diplomatic Ambitions of the BRIC State: Challenging the Hegemony of the West." *Journal of International Relations and Foreign Policy* 2, no. 2, pp. 1–18.

[20] Ferrari-Filho, F., and A. Spanakos. 2008. "Why Brazil has Not Grown: A Comparative Analysis of Brazilian and Chinese Economic Management." *Ensayos de Economía* 18, no. 32, p. 15.

[21] Bull, B., and Y. Kasahara. 2011. "Brazil and China: Partners or Competitors." *NorLARNet analysis*, pp. 9–10.

[22] Harden, B.E. 2014. "The Diplomatic Ambitions of the BRIC State: Challenging the Hegemony of the West." *Journal of International Relations and Foreign Policy* 2, no. 2, pp. 1–18.

[23] Nye, J.S. 2004. *Soft Power: The Means to Success in World Politics.* PublicAffairs.

[24] Military Spending Database. 2010. SIPRI. http://milexdata.sipri.org/ (accessed February 20, 2010).

[25] Bitencourt, L., and A.C. Vaz. 2009. Brazilian Strategic Culture. Finding Report, 5.

[26] Schläger, C. 2007. *Challenges for International Development Cooperation: The Case of Brazil.* Berlin: Friedrich Ebert Stiftung (FES).

[27] US Energy and Information Administration Statistics, EIA. 2010. http://eia. doe.gov/cabs/Russia/Background.html (March 1, 2010).

[28] Eitelhuber, N. 2009. "The Russian Bear: Russian Strategic Culture and What It Implies for the West." *Connections: The Quarterly Journal* 9, no. 1, p. 1.

[29] Ermarth, F.W. 2006. *Russia's Strategic Culture: The Past, Present and... in Transition?.* Washington, DC: U.S. Defense Threat Reduction Agency. http://fas.org/irp/agency/dod/dtra/russia.pdf

[30] Poddar, T., and E. Yi. 2007. "India's Rising Growth Potential." In *BRICs and Beyond*, ed. G. Sachs, 11. New York, NY: Global Economics Group.

[31] O'Neill, J., and T. Poddar. June 16, 2008. "Ten Things for India to Achieve its 2050 Potential." Goldman Sachs Global Economic Paper 169, 3–5. www2. goldmansachs.com/ideas/brics/howsolid-doc.pdf (accessed February 23, 2010).

[32] Menon, S. 2009. "Hostile Relations: India's Pakistan Dilemma." *Harvard International Review* 31, no. 3, p. 14.

[33] Bajoria, J., and E. Pan. 2010. "The US-India Nuclear Deal." *Council on Foreign Relations*, p. 5.

[34] Besada, H., and E. Tok. 2014. "South Africa in the BRICS: Soft Power Balancing and Instrumentalization." *Journal of International and Global Studies* 5, no. 2, pp. 76–96.

[35] Cravo, T.A., D.J. Hornsby, D. Nascimento, and S.J. Santos. 2014. African Emerging Powers. NOREF Report, 4.

[36] Draper, P., and S. Scholvin. 2012. The Economic Gateway to Africa? Geography, Strategy and South Africa's Regional Economic Relations.

[37] Misra-Dexter, N., and J. February, eds. 2010. *Testing Democracy: Which Way is South Africa Going?.* African Books Collective.

[38] The Economist. 2012. "Cry, the Beloved Country: South Africa's Sad Decline." October 20th–26th.

[39] The Top 10 Corruption Scandals In South Africa. https://buzzsouthafrica. com/here-are-the-top-10-corruption-scandals-in-south-africa/

CHAPTER 6

The Environmental Degradation

The Many Faces of Environmental Degradation

Environmental degradation is a broad concept that may refer to any undesirable and noxious changes made to the environment by human beings or natural causes. According to the United Nations International Strategy for Disaster Reduction, environmental degradation is "the reduction of the capacity of the environment to meet social and ecological objectives and needs" [1]. While the environmental degradation may be produced by natural causes, human beings and their economic activities, particularly after the Industrial Revolution, are known as the main culprits. The environmental degradation includes a wide range of phenomena such as climate change and global warming, gas emissions, air and water pollution, overpopulation and the subsequent resources overexploitation, deforestation, drought, solid waste pollution, and loss of biodiversity. The environmental degradation directly threats human life and indirectly implies several socioeconomic consequences like poverty, famine, war and armed conflicts, migration, and instability. The harmful consequences of environmental degradation are substantial particularly in developing countries where the risk of environmentally caused diseases is 15 times higher than in developed countries.

Greenhouse Gas Emissions

In the past 100 years, human beings have burned huge amounts of fossil fuels and have released large quantities of greenhouse gases into the atmosphere. The greenhouse emissions are those gases that trap heat in the atmosphere and thus cause global warming. The gas emissions include a variety of chemicals such as carbon dioxide, methane, nitrous oxide, and fluorinated gases. According to the United States Environment Protection Agency, the use of fossil fuel is the chief source of carbon dioxide, but deforestation, agricultural activities, and waste management all contribute to greenhouse gas emissions as well. The economic sectors or activities that lead to the generation of greenhouse emissions include electricity and heat production (25 percent), industry (21 percent), agriculture and forestry (24 percent), transportation (14 percent), and buildings construction (6 percent) [3]. Global carbon emissions from fossil fuels have extensively increased in the past 100 years, but the pace of surge has accelerated particularly since the 1970s. In the past three decades, the quantity of greenhouse emissions has increased constantly as other developing countries such as China and India have joined the club of industrialized countries. For instance, the global greenhouse emissions from human activities in 2010 reached 46 billion metric tons representing a 35 percent increase from 1990 [4]. For the same period, carbon dioxide that accounts for three-fourths of total global emissions increased by 42 percent. Overall, the emissions have increased by over 16 times between 1900 and 2008 and by about 1.5 times between 1990 and 2008. The energy production and consumption accounted for 71 percent of the total emissions in 2010. According to OECD's reports, global greenhouse gas emissions are expected to increase by about 37 percent between now and 2030, and by 52 percent between now and 2050 [5]. The same reports suggest that, in developing countries, the emissions growth will be significantly higher than in rich and developed countries (Figure 6.1 and 6.2). An interesting trend is

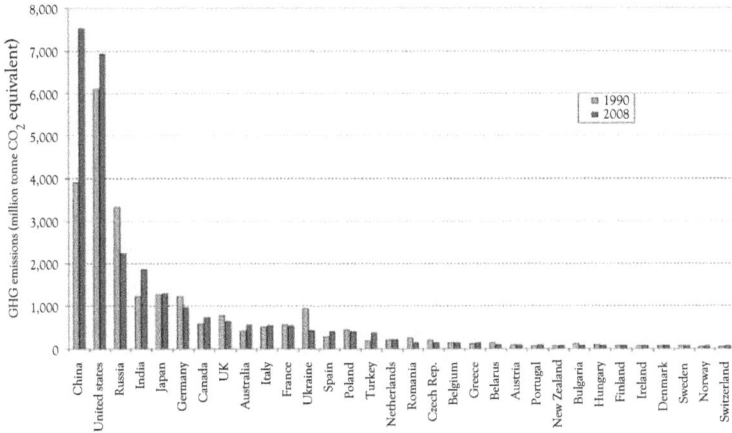

Figure 6.1 Greenhouse gas emissions by country (1990 and 2008)

Source: United Nations Framework Convention on Climate Change.

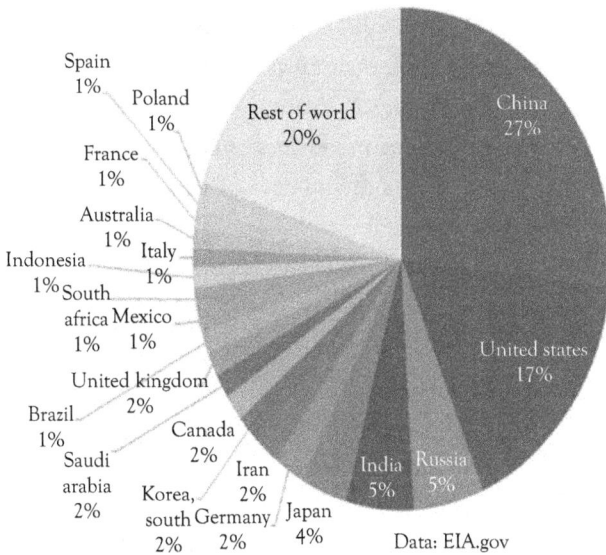

Figure 6.2 Carbon dioxide emissions by country (2011)

that, while developed countries will reduce their overall greenhouse gas emission, they will continue to have the highest emissions per capita [6]. The greenhouse emissions are growing much faster in Asia and Africa, but the main geographic sources of greenhouse gas emissions are concentrated in the United States, Asia, and Europe that accounted for 82 percent of total global emissions in 2011 [4]. According to the United States Environment Protection Agency, the top carbon dioxide emitters in 2008 were China, the United States, the EU, India, the Russian Federation, Japan, and Canada.

Air Pollution

Air pollution is one of the most flagrant features of the environmental degradation in many developing countries. Air pollution is a major environmental risk causing multiple health problems including respiratory infections, heart disease, and lung cancer. According to the World Health Organization (WHO), around 18,000 deaths per day or 6.5 million deaths per year are attributed to the air pollution making it the world's fourth-largest threat to human health [7]. More than 8 out of 10 people live in the urban areas where the air pollutants exceed the WHO's Air Quality Guidelines (WHO, 2006). Energy production and transport are recognized as the main sources of air pollution [1]. For every gallon of gasoline burned in a vehicle, 25 pounds of carbon dioxide and many other pollutants like carbon monoxides, sulfur dioxide, and nitrogen dioxide are produced [8]. As the number of cars in emerging countries such as China and India are increasing quickly, the air pollution in the urban areas is worsening at an accelerated pace.

Global Warming

Associated with the high levels of greenhouse gas emission is the climate change or global warming. Despite the skeptics' claims, it is scientifically accepted that climate change is a human-made phenomenon. The acceleration of climate warming observed throughout the 20th century is exceptional. Maximum temperatures, numbers of hot days, and the heat index have increased during the second half of the 20th century nearly in all continents [9]. In the past 100 years, the average temperature has climbed about 0.7°C (1.3°F) across the world. The 1980s, the 1990s, and the 2000s have been sequentially warmer at the earth's surface. According to the National Oceanic and Atmospheric Administration, the year 2014 was the hottest since 1880 [10]. The pace of climate warming is accelerating, but the Arctic regions are warming even faster than other parts of the planet [10]. The melting ice has led to sea levels rising at about two millimeters per year [10]. These patterns of global warming will continue in the next few decades, even if all greenhouse gas emissions were terminated now. The average temperature of the earth's surface is expected to increase between 1.4°C and 5.8°C by 2100 [9, 11]. The rising temperatures cause many changes in physical and biological systems across the world: the shrinkage of glaciers, changes in rainfall frequency, shifts in the growing season, early flowering of trees and emergence of insects, and shifts in the distribution ranges of plants and animals in response to changes in climatic conditions [9]. Further increase in the climate temperature could drastically disturb the balance of the world's ecosystems and cause additional irreparable and unpredictable transformations [12]. Some expected climate-induced events include heat waves, flash floods, tropical storms, infectious diseases, droughts, scarcity of renewable resources, sea-levels rise, and intensification of natural disasters [13]. Furthermore, the global warming is likely to adversely affect water and fertile soil and thus reduce the agricultural output.

Water Pollution

Water quality can be adversely affected by both human activities and natural factors. Nutrients, sediments, rising temperatures, heavy metals, nonmetallic toxins, pesticides, and biological organisms are among the most notable polluting causes of water resources [14]. Every day, 2 million tons of dirt and residential, industrial, and agricultural waste materials are released into the world's water resources, lakes, and rivers [15]. It is estimated that around 70 percent of industrial sewage in developing countries is discharged directly into natural waters [16]. The unsafe water supply results in 4 billion cases of diarrhea each year and causes 2.2 million deaths across the world. A combination of inadequate sewerage and open defecation that are widespread in Sub-Saharan Africa and India pose serious threats to water safety [17]. According to the WHO, almost 10 percent of the world's population or 768 million people do not have access to an improved source of water and one-third or 2.5 billion do not have secured access to adequate sanitation [18].

The problem of water pollution is not limited to developing countries. For instance, significant levels of pollution were found in the Japanese water supplies [19]. Due to the high levels of pollution, a significant portion of the world's water resources is not suitable for activities such as fishing and swimming. As the water reserves are becoming increasingly polluted and unusable, the groundwater resources are quickly dwindling due to overexploitation particularly in developing countries. At the same time, global water demand is estimated to surge by 55 percent by 2050 because of increasing demands from manufacturing, agriculture, and domestic use [20]. It is estimated that, by 2030, more than 5 billion people or 67 percent of the world population will be deprived of a connection to public sewerage [2].

Land Degradation

Land degradation takes different forms including deforestation, desertification, salinization, erosion, nutrient depletion, carbon loss, and loss of water [21]. Both human-related activities and natural factors may ruin the land, but only humans can cause the accelerated land degradation. Clearance of vegetative cover, soil erosion by wind or water, high-intensity rainfall, invasive species, chemical or bacterial pollution, drought, agricultural practices, urban expansion, and industrial activities are some typical causes of land degradation. For instance, by converting lands and forests into fertile farms for producing certain crops and livestock, farmers change the ecosystems, destroy wildlife, and erase vegetation. Furthermore, the accumulation of toxic substances like bad minerals, chemical fertilizers, and pesticides could destroy the soil's biological and chemical activities and deteriorate the quality of the soil. Across the world, over 20 percent of cultivated areas, 30 percent of forests, and 10 percent of grasslands have been hurt by land degradation, affecting about 1.5 billion people. Land degradation has touched half of agricultural lands over the last 50 years [22]. It is estimated that 75 percent of the drylands in Latin America and the Caribbean are currently under desertification or other forms of land degradation.

E-Waste

E-waste consists of discarded computers, cell phones, radios, televisions, refrigerators, washing machines, microwaves, and home appliances, which contain plastics, glass, and precious metals. E-waste is a rapidly grow-ing cause of environmental degradation. According to a United Nations University report, the amount of global E-waste reached 41.8 million tons in 2014 [23]. The United States and other developed countries that con-sume most of the world's electronic products generate most of the world's E-waste. However, the majority of the E-waste is shipped to developing countries. Since the United States has not ratified the Basel Convention, it ships almost 80 percent of its E-waste to developing parts of the world mainly to China, India, Pakistan, and Africa where they dispose of the E-waste using very primitive methods [24]. The trade of E-waste between rich and poor countries is beneficial for both parties: while the rich get rid of the waste, the poor recycle and resell the usable materials. The total value of the global E-waste was estimated around US$52 billion in 2014 consisting of 16,500 kilotons of iron, 1,900 kilotons of copper, and 300 tons of gold and significant amounts of silver, aluminum, palladium, and other useable materials.

In developing countries, vast amounts of E-waste materials are burned or dumped in the agricultural fields, irrigation canals, and along water-ways [25]. Burning E-waste results in solid and gaseous toxic chemicals, posing serious threats to the environment (Figure 6.3). The toxic materi-als may trickle into the ground and contaminate the soil and water, thus affecting the food chain including agricultural crops, fish, and livestock. Among the generated toxic materials, lead, copper, and cadmium are the three heavy metals that persist in the environment for a long time and are likely to be found in plants or in paddy fields [26]. The toxic materials can also go into the atmosphere when primitive E-waste salvaging meth-ods are used. The release of mercury and lead into the environment may

Figure 6.3 Most of the world's E-waste is exported to Africa, India, and China

cause neurological, respiratory, cardiovascular, renal, and skeletal damage in humans and other animals living in the areas nearby [27].

The adverse effects of E-waste on the natural environment are expected to sharply grow for multiple reasons. As countries get richer, the per capita use of cell phone, computer, and electronics also grows [25]. Over the next few years, the developing countries will make up the bulk of the electronic sales as they draw near to the developed countries [28]. Unlike other products, the electronics have shorter life cycles and higher rates of obsolescence that make them rapidly disposable [25]. The tech companies are not only constantly innovating and replacing the old products, but also are using some planned obsolescence manufacturing techniques to entice consumers to purchase the latest products and dispose of the old ones. The combination of these factors pushes consumers to replace their electronics unnecessarily, thus generating more E-waste.

The Drivers of Environmental Degradation

Human beings are the number one culprit of environmental degradation. Overpopulation, urbanization, energy production and consumption, business activities, agriculture, industrialization, and transport directly or indirectly contribute to the environmental degradation. The world has experienced a steep rise in the global population in the second half of the 20th century from 2.5 billion in 1950 to 6 billion in 2000, and 7.5 billion in 2017 [5]. Despite some slowdown in the world population growth, the number of human beings on the planet will increase in the next decades. The world population is expected to exceed 9 billion in 2038 [29]. About 90 percent of the population growth will be concentrated in low- and middle-income countries. The fastest-growing region will be Sub-Saharan Africa, and the largest number of people will be added in Asia, particularly in the Indian subcontinent [5]. This huge and fast increase of human populations on the planet implies devastating implications for the environment. Furthermore, the effects of population growth on the environmental degradation are amplified by urbanization. Three decades ago, only 38 percent of the world's population lived in cities, but the share of urbanized population exceeded 50 percent in 2015. The number of the world's urban dwellers is growing fast and large cities are attracting even more people. By 2050, the share of the urban population is expected to reach 67 percent. Most of the growth in urban population will be concentrated in developing countries and in megacities in Southern and Eastern Asia. This pace of urbanization puts an additional strain on the environment through land degradation, destruction, and fragmentation of natural habitats, water pollution, increases in greenhouse gas emissions, and air pollution [5]. Likewise, building and demolition activities in urban centers generate a lot of debris and solid trash, consuming almost one-third to one-half of the world's commodities. The extent of environmental degradation will be particularly significant in developing countries as they are marked by high birth rates and urbanization growth.

Manufacturing is still an important sector of the economic production primarily in emerging countries. Currently, the share of manufacturing is estimated at about 40 percent of the world output. Manufacturing activities rely on the use of different types of resources, consume energy, and generate large amounts of solid or gaseous waste. Due to a manufacturing boom in emerging markets, base and precious metals, biomass, woods, and materials are in high demand. Similarly, global resource extraction has increased vastly in the past decades, from 40 billion ton in 1980 to 58 billion ton in 2005 and is expected to increase to 80 billion ton in 2020 [2].

Agriculture and fishing are other economic sectors that put pressure on the planet's resources and cause the environmental degradation. There is a growing demand for every kind of food because not only human beings are growing in number, but also they are eating more. Furthermore, as people in emerging countries attain at the economic prosperity, they tend to consume more protein and meat products. Not surprisingly, the livestock sector is one of the fastest-growing parts of the agricultural economy [30]. The shift from cereal to meat consumption could cause an increase in agricultural production by roughly 50 percent between 2005 and 2030 [2].

Energy and transport sectors are other major contributors to environmental degradation as they generate greenhouse gas and other pollutants. The global primary energy consumption is estimated to increase by 1.8 percent annually [5]. In the recent years, renewable energies like solar and wind have been promulgated, but the traditional energy resources including fossil fuels and nuclear are still very popular. The total share of fossil fuels in energy consumption is supposed to remain constant at about 85 percent at least until 2030 when it may fall to reach 80 percent in 2050 [2].

The Consequences of Environmental Degradation

First, the environmental degradation has negative effects on human health. Evidently, the phenomena such as air and water pollution, land degradation, and greenhouse gas emissions seriously affect our health and well-being. Water pollution alone is responsible for more than 2 million deaths across the world annually. Likewise, poor air quality causes more than 6.5 million deaths annually and millions of respiratory diseases like pneumonia and asthma [7]. The presence of chlorofluorocarbons and hydro chlorofluorocarbons in the atmosphere causes the ozone layer depletion that will emit harmful radiations back to the earth. Chemical and bacterial pollutants enter our food chains and harm produces from fish, meat, and chicken to vegetables, fruits, and beans. The various toxic wastes and harmful chemicals derived from industry, agriculture, and transport cause illnesses and death across the globe. Furthermore, desertification, deforestation, and salinization destroy the natural land cover, deplete the ozone layer, and increase the risk of skin cancer and eye disease.

Poverty is another inevitable consequence of environmental degradation. Across the globe and particularly in developing countries, poverty is related to soil erosion, desertification, water scarcity, and erratic climate changes that cause poor crop yields. Desertification, land degradation, and a shortage of fresh water have negative effects on food production, increase the risks of flooding and droughts, and exacerbate food insecurity particularly in the least developed countries [12]. Additionally, the environmental degradation could result in turmoil and conflict where the resources are already scarce. Due to environmental degradation, the normal business activities could cost the world economy up to 20 percent of global GDP per year [12]. Global warming and the ensuing rising sea levels could destroy the buildings and infrastructures at the coastal zones that are containing about one-fifth of the world's population. Many large cities and important ports are located by the sea or in river deltas and their populations, infrastructures, industries, ports, oil refineries, and transport systems are at the risk of rising sea levels. Similarly, rising sea levels threaten populations on small islands in the Indian Ocean, the Caribbean, and the Pacific [13]. The densely populated regions in Africa, Asia, and South America are mostly exposed to the risks of climate change because they have limited resources to adapt themselves to the climate change. Even some regions of developed countries in the Western Europe and North America will be affected severely [31].

Rising sea levels and the submergence of large coastal zones may result in territorial disputes over land and maritime borders. Global warming may cause other opportunities and threats in the polar regions and thus trigger competition and conflict among the concerned nations. At the same time, desertification and deforestation could cause clashes over territory leading to political instability and conflict across the planet [12]. Due to water scarcity/pollution or desertification, a large number of affected people have to migrate to other regions or countries. According to the United Nations predictions, there will be millions of environmental migrants by 2020 [12]. The poor and developing parts of Asia, South America, Africa, and the Middle East that have higher birth rates are more vulnerable to environmental degradation and are expected to produce a lot of environmental migrants. By contrast, Europe, North America, and Australia are more likely to receive such environmentally induced migrants.

Facing the horrible effects of environmental degradation, many national and local governments fall short of providing basic services to their citizens. The inability of governments to meet the needs of their populations could generate more frustration and tensions. As the effects of environmental damage become more flagrant, the level of cooperation among nation-states seems necessary. The highly affected nations may blame those responsible for climate change and, as a result, the resentment in the international community could increase. The friction could be especially significant between the developed and developing countries that have diverging economic structures and cultural values [12].

Degradation of the environment under all its forms is responsible for a continuous damage to natural ecosystems and a massive extinction of many living species [32]. The current environmental degradation has resulted in permanent changes in the functioning and status of the earth's ecosystems that ultimately cause a substantial reduction of the biodiversity. In a study conducted by the World Bank, 15 out of 24 ecosystems were degraded [33]. For many living species, the rising temperatures are not tolerable. For instance, an increase of 1°C may be sufficient to extinct 10 percent of land species [33]. Similarly, an increase of 4°C could destroy as much as 30 percent of land species [34]. Therefore, by transforming ecological systems, global warming will severely reduce biodiversity in the next decades.

While environmental degradation affects the entire humanity, those people in poor and developing countries will suffer most, as they are dependent on sectors such as agriculture and fisheries [11]. Furthermore, the capacity of developing countries in adapting to climate change is very limited. Generally, we can say that the least developed countries in the tropical and subtropical areas will be the most vulnerable to the destructive effects of environmental degradation. By contrast, the rich and advanced economies will be able to take measures to mitigate the negative effects of climate change. Africa is for the most part vulnerable to the effects of environmental degradation and may lose between 2 and 7 percent of its GDP due to increased risks of droughts, floods, and pest outbreaks [35]. Currently, North Africa and the Sahel are tackling with growing problems such as drought, water scarcity, soil erosion, and loss of arable land. The Nile Delta in Egypt with millions of habitats is at risk from sea-level rise, soil erosion, and salinization of arable land. In the Horn of Africa, Darfur, and Southern Africa climate change, drought, soil erosion, and food shortages are responsible for increasing levels of ethnic tensions and conflicts [12]. Likewise, the Middle East is experiencing droughts, reduced rainfall, sand storms, air pollution, land degradation, and rising temperatures. Around two-thirds of Arab countries are dependent on sources outside their borders for water [12]. There are tensions over access to water among many Middle Eastern countries like Jordan, Israel, Palestine, Turkey, Iraq, and Syria. Over time and with the growing trend of environmental degradation, we may expect higher levels of water-related conflict. Substantial drops in fresh water resources in the Middle Eastern countries such as Turkey, Iran, Iraq, Syria, and Saudi Arabia could severely affect their sociopolitical stability [12].

South Asia is a region vulnerable to sea-level rise. Due to a high population density, the lives and belongings of millions of habitats are at risk. It is interesting to note that more than 40 percent of Asia's population or almost 2 billion people live within 60 km from the coastline [12]. Furthermore, a large portion of Asia's population is still extremely poor and relies on traditional agriculture. Therefore, any kind of damage to agricultural productivity due to water quality, soil erosion, and climate change will have destructive effects on the subsistence of billions of people. It is evident that further strain on natural resources, water, and arable land will result in mass migration, higher levels of conflict, and sociopolitical turmoil. Central Asia is another region vulnerable to the effects of environmental degradation. Most of the Central Asian countries are landlocked and rely on limited water resources for agriculture. The reduction in rainfall, shortage of water resources, and soil erosion are already affecting Kyrgyzstan and Tajikistan. Many coastal parts of Latin American and Caribbean countries are exposed to the sea-level increases. Furthermore, reduction in rainfall and the waning glaciers could affect water availability for human consumption, agriculture, and energy generation in much of Latin America. These changes may imply adverse consequences for food security and local economies.

References

[1] Tyagi, S., N. Garg, and R. Paudel. 2014. "Environmental Degradation: Causes and Consequences." *European Researcher* Series A, nos. 8–2, pp. 1491–98.

[2] OECD. 2008. OECD Environmental Outlook to 2030. Organisation for Economic Co-Operation and Development, Paris.

[3] Melillo, J.M., T.T. Richmond, and G. Yohe. 2014. Climate Change Impacts in the United States. Third National Climate Assessment.

[4] UNEP (United Nations Environment Programme). 2013. *Global Environment Outlook 2000*, 1 vols. Routledge.

[5] Ruta, G. 2010. "Monitoring Environmental Sustainability Trends, Challenges, and the Way Forward." The World Bank Group. accessed 06/10/2017 from https://google.com/url?sa=t&rct=j&q=&esrc=s&source=web&cd=1& ved=0ahUKEwjjgZLBo4nVAhWl7YMKHWc0CrwQFggmMAA&url=ht tp%3A%2F%2Fsiteresources.worldbank.org%2FEXTENVSTRATEGY% 2FResources%2F6975692-1289855310673%2F20101209-Monitoring-Environmental-Sustainability.pdf&usg=AFQjCNGbWcJ1qZryp8sdBEI-66kYZYBQeQ&cad=rja

[6] Arto, I., and E. Dietzenbacher. 2014. "Drivers of the Growth in Global Greenhouse Gas Emissions." *Environmental Science & Technology* 48, no. 10, pp. 5388–94.

[7] World Energy Outlook Special Report. 2016. Energy and Air Pollution, available at https://iea.org/publications/freepublications/publication/weo-2016-special-report-energy-and-air-pollution.html

[8] Donohoe, M. 2003. "Causes and Health Consequences of Environmental Degradation and Social Injustice." *Social Science & Medicine* 56, no. 3, pp. 573–87.

[9] Kampa, M., and E. Castanas. 2008. "Human Health Effects of Air Pollution." *Environmental Pollution* 151, no. 2, pp. 362–67.

[10] Harris, J.M., and B. Roach. 2007. *The Economics of Global Climate Change.* Global Development and Environment Institute Tufts University.

[11] Solomon, S, ed. 2007. *Climate Change 2007-The Physical Science Basis: Working Group I Contribution to the Fourth Assessment Report of the IPCC,* 4 vols. Cambridge University Press.

[12] Holden, E., K. Linnerud, and D. Banister. 2014. "Sustainable Development: Our Common Future Revisited." *Global Environmental Change* 26, pp. 130–39.

[13] Theisen, O.M., N.P. Gleditsch, and H. Buhaug. 2013. "Is Climate Change a Driver of Armed Conflict?." *Climatic Change* 117, no. 3, pp. 613–25.

[14] Carr, G.M., and J.P. Neary. 2008. *Water Quality for Ecosystem and Human Health*, 2nd ed. United Nations Environment Programme Global Environment Monitoring System. Retrieved July 14, 2009 from http://gemswater.org/ publications/pdfs/water_quality_human_health.pdf

[15] The World Health Organization, Drinking-water, Fact sheet , Updated July 2017. http:/who.int/mediacentre/factsheets/fs391/en/

[16] Water, U.N., M.P.H.A. Mobile, and P.T.A. Toilet. 2014. World Water Day.

[17] The World Bank 2010. Environment Strategy 2010: Analytical Background Papers (English). http://documents.worldbank.org/curated/en/355 491468333022953/Environment-strategy-2010-analytical-background-papers

[18] WHO/UNICEF. 2013. Progress on Sanitation and Drinking-Water 2013 Update: Joint Monitoring Programme for Water Supply and Sanitation.

[19] UNEP (United Nations Environment Programme). 2013. *Global Environment Outlook 2000,* 1 vols. Routledge.

[20] Marchal, V., R. Dellink, D. Van Vuuren, C. Clapp, J. Chateau, B. Magné, and J. van Vliet. 2011. "OECD Environmental Outlook to 2050." *Organization for Economic Co-operation and Development.*

[21] Wood, S., K. Sebastian, and S.J. Scherr. 2000. "Soil Resource Condition." In *Pilot Analysis of Global Ecosystems (Page)*, 45–54. Washington, DC: IFPRI and World Resources Institute.

[22] Bossio, D., A. Noble, J. Pretty, and F. Penning de Vries. August 2004. "Reversing Land and Water Degradation: Trends and 'Bright Spot' Opportunities." In SIWI/CA Seminar, Stockholm, Sweden Vol. 21.

[23] Baldé, C.P. 2015. *The Global E-waste Monitor 2014: Quantities, Flows and Resources*. United Nations University.

[24] Owens, M. 2015. Disposal of E-Waste and Its Impacts on the Ecosystem.

[25] Byster, L., S. Westervelt, R. Gutierrez, S. Davis, A. Hussain, and M. Dutta. 2002. "Exporting Harm: The High-Tech Trashing of Asia." In ed. J. Puckett, 3 vols. Seattle: Basel Action Network.

[26] Luo, C., C. Lui, Y. Wang, X. Liu, F. Li, G. Zhang, and X. Li. 2011. "Heavy Metals Contamination in Soils and Vegetables Near an E-waste Processing Site, South China." *Journal of Hazardous Materials* 186, pp. 481–90.

[27] Environmental Protection Agency, Basic Information. April 14, 2014. Retrieved April 28, 2015, from http://epa.gov/solidwaste/nonhaz/municipal/wte/basic.htm

[28] Van der Meulen, R. March 19, 2015. "Gartner Says Global Devices Shipments to Grow 2.8 Percent in 2015." Retrieved May 1, 2015, from http://gartner.com/newsroom/id/3010017

[29] Bloom, D.E. 2011. "7 Billion and Counting." *Science* 333, no. 6042, pp. 562–69.

[30] FAO (Food and Agriculture Organization). 2009. The State of Food and Agriculture 2009. Food and Agriculture Organization of the United Nations, Rome.

[31] Mann, M.E. 2009. "Do Global Warming and Climate Change Represent a Serious Threat to Our Welfare and Environment?." *Social Philosophy and Policy* 26, no. 2, pp. 193–230.

[32] Rockström, J., W. Steffen, K. Noone, Å. Persson, F.S. Chapin III, E. Lambin, T. Lenton, M. Scheffer, C. Folke, H.J. Schellnhuber, and B. Nykvist. 2009. "Planetary Boundaries: Exploring the Safe Operating Space for Humanity." *Ecology and Society* 14, no. 2.

[33] World Bank 2010. *World Development Report 2010: Development and Climate Change*. Washington, DC: World Bank.

[34] UNDP (United Nations Development Programme). 2008. "Human Development Report 2007/2008." *Fighting Climate Change: Human Solidarity in a Divided World*. New York: UNDP.

[35] World Bank. 2008. *Climate Change: Adaptation and Mitigation in Development Programs: A Practical Guide*. Washington, DC: World Bank.

CHAPTER 7

Challenges to Security and Governance

The Hybrid Warfare

Since the turn of the century, we are witnessing the rise of a new type of conflict known as "hybrid warfare." The North Atlantic Treaty Organization (NATO) has used the concept of hybrid warfare as an umbrella term including various adverse circumstances and actions [1]. We may suggest that the hybrid warfare is a response to an emerging group of global threats that go beyond the traditional area of any single government agency [2]. Indeed, the complexity of international environment implies that conflicts and armed encounters cannot be won by military means alone. Therefore, the hybrid war may consist of different modes of fighting such as conventional capabilities, irregular tactics and formations, terrorist acts, indiscriminate violence and coercion, and criminal disorder [3]. The hybrid war is a war without rules and restrictions transcending the limits of the battlefield, the weapon, the military, and the state [4]. The hybrid warfare may involve the use of a very comprehensive and nuanced variety of military activities, resources, programs, and applications. In other words, in a hybrid fighting, the military force is only a small part and war operations include various paramilitary, military and civilian, direct and hidden actions that can be conducted by both state and nonstate actors [3]. In the hybrid war, the social and institutional softness, in conjunction with the military weakness, is targeted. The conflict in Ukraine in the past five years can be categorized as a good example of a hybrid war [1]. Russia's war in Ukraine capitalizes on multiple acts such as conducting covert small military operations, creating criminal disorder, hijacking social media, collecting intelligence, distributing malware, and supporting local militias to deal with the West as a much stronger rival [5]. Similarly, the conflict between Israel and the Lebanese Hezbollah in 2006 is a typical example of a hybrid warfare as it included both state and nonstate actors, conventional military power, as well as political, social, diplomatic, and informational components and operations [6]. Due to its hybridization, there is no distinctive and politically well-defined line between war and peace [7, 1]. The hybrid wars are generally marked by their long durations as they could last for several decades. Furthermore, the hybrid wars require strong leadership, well-informed decision making, and comprehensive strategies that enable the application of all facets of state power to achieving a suitable resolution to the conflict [2].

The Rise of Asymmetrical Warfare

In a globalized, complex, and interdependent world, asymmetrical warfare is becoming increasingly an important type of rivalry. Asymmetrical warfare can be considered as any type of fighting that uses comparative advantages against an opponent's weaknesses [8]. In an asymmetrical warfare, "have-nots" undertake the warfare against "haves" by applying their specific advantages against the weaknesses of a much stronger adversary [9]. For that reason, asymmetrical warfare is a war that is not defensible with a conventional military force. In the past decades, the chances of full-fledged conventional conflicts among large nation-states have diminished. At the same time, the incidences of asymmetrical conflicts among nation-states or between nation-states and nonstates actors have increased. For instance, in the past 20 years, more American citizens have been killed in asymmetrical warfare than in conventional military battles [10]. What makes the asymmetrical warfare difficult is that it is carried out by the individuals or groups that are not directly connected to a state or nation. Furthermore, the targets of asymmetrical warfare are not limited to military facilities and may include a wide range of political, economic, and cultural interests. The asymmetrical attacks often seek to cause psychological and emotional damage [8]. The asymmetrical attackers may use various techniques and devices such as airplanes, cars, trucks, postal systems, computers, chemicals, viruses, and biological weapons. Because of rapid technological innovations, the asymmetrical attacks are becoming constantly more frequent and more damaging. Considering these various and complex features, winning the asymmetrical warfare is extremely difficult.

Cyber-Attack and Cyber-Espionage

Cyber-attacks may include any intended actions to change, interrupt, or destroy computer systems and the associated information and programs [11]. Some cyber-attacks may be categorized as cyber-espionage as they do not interrupt or destroy the computer networks; rather they aim at stealing information for intelligence purposes. Depending on the importance of targeted computer networks, the effects of cyber-attacks could vary from interrupting a website to disruption or even destruction of critical information systems. The importance of cyber-security is continuing to grow exponentially as cyberspace is expanding to many aspects of our lives. Indeed, the complexity of information systems is growing much faster than the technical capability to protect them [12]. The most expected targets of cyber-attacks are critical networks that if interrupted would disrupt normal life and would inflict significant financial, technological, or human loss [13]. Cyber-attacks may be used to interrupt financial and air traffic control systems, commit financial fraud, steal corporate information and intellectual property, and penetrate into state and military secret services. It is estimated that, in 2008, cyber-attacks in the United States have resulted in a loss of intellectual property of more than $1 trillion [11]. Considering their significant implications, some types of cyber-attacks may ignite political tensions and escalate to full-fledged international conflicts. Both state and nonstate adversaries who are able to acquire the required competence may perpetrate cyber-attacks. The cyber-attackers could include anybody who possesses the technical capabilities to exploit the computer systems' vulnerabilities [14]. Cyber-attackers constitute diverse groups ranging from petty and organized criminals to state-backed institutions, fundamentalist religious groups, terrorists, and pressure groups. Indeed, some cyber-attackers have been as young as 13 years old. For these reasons, it is very easy to launch cyber-attacks and it is extremely difficult to track, identify, and prosecute the perpetrators. Another problem with the cyber-attack and cyber-espionage is that the terrorists do not need to travel to enemy's territory, rather they can launch their attacks via the Internet even when they are thousands of miles away. Unlike other types of warfare, it is not clear who should be held accountable for a cyber-attack. Even when the cyber-attack is attributed to a nation, it is very difficult to decide about a proportionate riposte or punishment. Consequently, cyber-attack is the perfect asymmetrical warfare as it allows the weak to attack the strong with little weapons and with very little fear of vengeance [8]. In contrast to a cyber-attack that disrupts computer networks, a cyber-espionage often does not affect the normal operation of computers, rather aims at stealing valuable information from the adversaries' computers and servers. As such, cyber-espionage may produce a high return for a small amount of investment. Indeed, a few competent hackers may crawl into computer networks for extremely valuable business or military secrets [14].

The Global Terrorism

The global terrorism is a new phenomenon that may refer to terrorist operations carried out in multiple nations or locations. As the terminology suggests, the global terrorism is a by-product of globalization and the recent advances in telecommunication and transport. Globalization has distorted our commonly held concepts of space and time and has turned our planet into a global village such that every person is in constant and close touch with the rest of the world [40, 41, 42]. Unlike old terrorism, the global terrorism has capitalized on global forces to create the diffuse, decentralized, and nebulous organizational structures that can simultaneously perform violent operations around the world. In contrast to old terrorist groups that typically were defined in a geographical area, the global terrorism is not confined to a particular geographical location. Al-Qaeda and Islamic

State of Iraq and Syria (ISIS) are prime examples of the global terrorist organizations that constitute of decentralized global networks of Islamic extremists united by a fundamentalist ideology [15]. Unlike the nationalist and leftist characters of the 1960s through 1980s, the new global terrorism is inspired by religious and spiritual visions [16]. During the cold war, not a single terrorist group in the world could be categorized as religiously motivated, but by the mid-1990s, the religiously motivated terrorism constituted one-third of all terrorist groups ranging from Christians in the United States, Jewish extremists in the West Bank, the Buddhist in Asia, and various Muslim terrorist groups across the world [17].

Currently, the majority of religiously motivated terrorist groups are inspired by an extremist version of Islam and by what they see as a command of God [18]. Religion is central to their terrorist operations because it offers many advantages. Religions in general and the Islamic faith, in particular, can guide in-group morality and out-group hatred, minimize the fear of death by spreading the belief in an afterlife reward, and effectively recruit the youth [19]. Al-Qaeda, ISIS, and other Jihadist terrorist groups openly believe in pursuing a divine mission through violence. They call upon their followers to wage a sacred war against nonbelievers including the Westerners across the world, in order to establish a radical religious state, an Islamic caliphate governed by Sharia law. It is important to note that the Islamic terrorism does not exempt ordinary Muslims from their violence. Indeed, most of the terror attacks perpetrated by Al-Qaeda, Taliban, and ISIS have targeted Muslims in countries such as Iraq, Afghanistan, Turkey, Yemen, and Syria. As such, the Islamic terrorism is primarily a cultural and ideological war that targets the outside world including Muslims, non-Muslims, Westerners, and all those who do not share their strict worldview. In contrast to the old terrorism, the global terrorism does not necessarily intend to assassinate or remove political leaders, rather targets ordinary citizens and uses psychological warfare as an effective strategy [25]. The subsequent nervousness in the targeted population leads to political pressure that may correspond to the terrorists' interests [21]. The global terrorism seeks to intensify the public's fear by conducting random attacks at soft targets instead of political or military figures. Therefore, globalization and the associated improvements in telecommunication have helped the global terrorism send and amplify its message of intimidation to the general public through the media coverage.

Some terrorist groups in developing countries blame globalization for their local problems and perceive the globalized economy as a continuation of imperialist practices aimed at exploiting and surrendering their countries or cultures. They believe that globalization as a corrupting western project is undermining their culture and their way of life. In that sense, the global terrorism may be described as a backlash against the globalization phenomenon itself. It seems that there is a direct relationship between globalization and the level of terrorist incidents. For instance, the number of terrorist attacks has increased significantly after the cold war during the 1990s and 2000s [15]. As the different parts of the world are becoming interconnected and thus interdependent, we may expect further increases in the number of terrorist incidents.

The collapse of the World Trade Center buildings, the destruction of parts of the Pentagon, and the death of more than 3,000 civilians on 9/11 may be viewed as a turning point in the development of global terrorism. The world leaders recognized the destructive power of Jihadi fundamentalist groups and implemented some hefty security measures [21]. What makes the Jihadi terrorism particularly vicious is its reliance on suicide attackers who by sacrificing their lives choose the time and place of their attacks to maximize damage. The global terrorist groups have secret relations with some states and influential individuals who provide them with financial, logistical, and military support. Furthermore, some terrorist organizations are relying on criminal activities such as drug trafficking, counterfeiting, kidnapping, human trafficking, and extortion to raise money for their subsistence [20]. In general, globalization has helped funding and coordination of Islamist fundamentalist and terrorist groups around the world. For instance, Al-Qaeda and ISIS have financial and operational links with other Islamic groups around the world. Boko Haram is based in Nigeria, but coordinated operations from Mali, and received funding and training from a UK-based Al-Muntada Trust Fund [20].

In the past several years, the terrorist organizations like Al-Qaeda and ISIS have aimed at spreading their ideologies through mosques, Islamic charities, community centers, and the Internet. The Internet websites, blogs, and social media overcome the geographic barriers and serve as forums to meet, recruit, and radicalize new members. The goal of these terrorist organizations is to attract new members particularly young Muslim immigrants and converts to Islam in Europe and North America. Since the homegrown terrorists live and work in the Western countries, they are able to effectively infiltrate their local communities and carry out destructive terrorist operations [21]. The new waves of terrorism pose a serious threat to the liberal democratic values in the western countries because they have to curb the citizen's freedoms to enhance the public security and thwart potential terror attacks. After the recent terror attacks in France, the UK, and Germany, many western countries had to restrict the basic rights like the freedom of movement, freedom of speech, and individual privacy [22].

The collapse of the Soviet Union in 1991 resulted in a decrease in the conflict and friction between communist and capitalistic ideologies, but it resulted in the rise of fundamentalist ideologies in some Islamic countries. Similar to communism, the Islamic fundamentalism seeks to offer a social, cultural, economic, and political alternative to the liberal democracies. The Islamic fundamentalist groups promote their political agenda by taking advantage of the populations' frustrations in the Middle East, North Africa, and South Asia where people are suffering from strained economies, high youth unemployment, and oppressive leaderships [26]. In the recent years, the Islamic fundamentalist groups have benefited from the Western military interventions in the Islamic countries notably Afghanistan, Iraq, Libya, Pakistan, and Syria to blame the Western liberal democracies for the destabilization of their home countries. It is widely believed that abject poverty and lack of education are the main factors underlying the rise of religious fundamentalism [27]. Therefore, the population growth and stagnant economies in many Islamic countries may aggravate the religious fundamentalism.

The Fragile and Failing States

The state strength is the extent to which a state is capable of providing basic socioeconomic and political services especially physical security, legitimate institutions, economic management, and social welfare [28].

Strong states effectively control their territories and provide the full range of socioeconomic and political services to their citizens. They protect their land from any kind of violence, guarantee political freedom and civil liberties, and make environments favorable to economic growth [29]. Not all states are strong enough. For instance, some states such as Afghanistan are struggling to keep a control on the use of military force. Others may lack the legitimate power to govern institutions and protect the basic rights and freedoms. Some others like Zimbabwe are virtually incapable of managing economic and fiscal matters of their nations. The weak states may become "failing states" if the conditions deteriorate and if they fall short of delivering goods in the four areas of physical security, legitimate political institutions, economic management, and social welfare. Some weak states may fail when they lose foreign support [30]. The main characteristic of the failed states is the loss of control of their territory or the monopoly on the legitimate use of military power. The loss of legitimate authority and the inability to provide public services are other characteristics of the failed states. Very often, the institutions of the failed states are impaired, their infrastructure is damaged, and their education and health care become unavailable to the public [33].

Foreign Policy and The Brookings Institution have recently developed indexes to measure the state weakness. The Foreign Policy Index relies on 12 dimensions to measure the fragility of world states, that is, demographic pressures, refugees and internally displaced persons, group grievance, human flight, uneven development, poverty and economic decline, legitimacy of the state, public services, human rights, security apparatus, factionalized elites, and external intervention. In 2016, 179 states were included in the Fragile States Index, of which 22 were classified as "Alert" and 16 were classified as "High Alert" or "Very High Alert." Among "High Alert" or "Very High Alert" states we can find Somalia, South Sudan, Central African Republic, Sudan, Yemen, Syria, Chad, Congo, Afghanistan, Haiti, Iraq, Guinea, Nigeria, Pakistan, Burundi, and Zimbabwe (see Table 7.1.). Many of these fragile or failed states are war-torn countries such as Somalia, Yemen, Syria, Afghanistan, and Iraq, which have experienced foreign invasion or civil war. State failure is becoming the source of a wide range of problems including regional instability, weapons proliferation, narcotics trafficking, and terrorism [33]. Some of

Table 7.1 The top 30 fragile states in 2017 according to Foreign Policy magazine (http://foreignpolicy.com)

1	South Sudan	11	Haiti	21	Côte d'Ivoire
2	Somalia	12	Guinea	22	Kenya
3	The Central African Republic	13	Nigeria	23	Libya
4	Yemen	13	Zimbabwe	24	Uganda
5	Sudan	15	Ethiopia	25	Myanmar
6	Syria	16	Guinea-Bissau	26	Cameroon
7	The Democratic Republic of the Congo	17	Burundi	27	Liberia
8	Chad	17	Pakistan	28	Mauritania
9	Afghanistan	19	Eritrea	29	The Republic of the Congo
10	Iraq	20	Niger	30	North Korea

the failed states such as Iraq, Afghanistan, Yemen, Syria, Libya, Somalia, and Sudan have become safe havens for terrorist groups that can use large territories within these countries to generate revenue, recruit supporters, construct training complexes, and store weapons and ammunitions. The failed states pose a significant security threat not only to their neighbors but also to the developed western countries that are becoming increasingly affected by the influx of migrants and terrorist attacks on their land. The state failure or fragility has some pernicious effects for the fight against corruption, the promotion of human rights, good governance, the rule of law, religious tolerance, environmental protection, child labor, gender equality, and more importantly the socioeconomic development [31]. Therefore, the failed states contribute to a long list of threats to the world security: poverty, disease, famine, migration influx, global terrorism, organized crime, weapons proliferation, religious intolerance, and the outbreak of violence, ethnic cleansing, and genocide [33].

Transnational Organized Crime

Transnational organized crime is a huge and lucrative business that has been growing in the past two decades. It is very difficult to measure the size of transnational organized crime, but revenues generated from major criminal activities are estimated to vary between US$1.6 trillion and $2.2 trillion per year, which is equivalent to around 7 percent of the world's exports of merchandise [37]. Transnational organized crime has hugely benefited from globalization and advances in telecommunication, transport, and international trade in the past three decades. Furthermore, the collapse of the Soviet Union and the subsequent transition from the centrally planned to the market-based economy in the Eastern Europe provided huge opportunities for transnational organized criminal organizations [35]. Transnational organized crime is a dynamic industry motivated by exorbitant levels of illicit profit that adapts to all markets and societies. It constantly reinvents itself and overcomes the legal, linguistic, and geographical boundaries.

The global drug trafficking is the most lucrative business for transnational organized criminals with an estimated annual value of US$426 billion to $652 billion in 2014 [37]. Cannabis, cocaine, opiates, and amphetamine-type stimulants are responsible for the largest shares of drug trafficking. While amphetamine-type stimulants and cannabis are produced in various countries, cocaine and heroin are produced mainly in South America and Afghanistan [37]. Cocaine is transported from Colombia to Mexico or Central America by sea and then onward by land to the United States and Canada. The size of cocaine market in the United States was estimated around US$38 billion in 2008. The European cocaine market is growing in the recent years and was estimated at US$34 billion in 2008 [36]. The global market value of heroin is estimated about US$55 billion annually. Most of the world's heroin is produced in Afghanistan and is transported to customers in the Russian Federation and Western Europe.

Human trafficking is becoming one of the most lucrative criminal activities in the recent years. Human trafficking refers to all activities involving involuntary or compelled control or exploitation of human beings. It can include involuntary servitude, sexual exploitation, slavery, debt bondage, and forced labor. The victims of human trafficking are often physically, sexually, and emotionally abused [38]. According to the International Labor Organization an estimated 21 million men, women, and children around the world are victims of human trafficking generating about US$150.2 billion in profits annually [37]. Almost half of the human trafficking takes place in the Asia-Pacific region with an estimated 12 million victims. While human trafficking could happen within one single country, it is mainly a cross-national business. According to a recent study by the United Nations Office on Drugs and Crime, the victims of human trafficking can be found in 137 countries. Almost two-thirds of the human trafficking victims are women and 79 percent of them are exposed to sexual exploitation [36]. Very often, the traffickers and victims are of the same nationality. In order to target their victims, the traffickers use employment agencies in the Eastern Europe and Asia, and social and family connections in Africa. Alongside human trafficking, organ trafficking is considered a very lucrative business for criminal organizations, generating between US$840 million and $1.7 billion annually [37]. The most trafficked organs include kidney, liver, heart, lung, and pancreas and are used in more than 12,000 illegal or legal transplants. The donors often may participate willingly or under coercion to sell their organs. For instance, organ traffickers may force migrants and refugees to sell kidneys to pay for passage to Europe [37].

Human smuggling is another form of organized crime that consists of assisting people to enter a country illegally. Refugees in war-torn countries and workers in poor countries of Asia, Africa, and South America may pay huge amounts of money and risk their lives to access opportunities in the more prosperous countries. For that reason, they rely on organized criminals to assist them to reach their destinations clandestinely. Migrants' relatives in the country of origin or in the destination often finance the payment to smugglers. There are two main flows of human smuggling: from Latin America to North America and from Africa to Europe. An estimated 3 million Latin Americans are smuggled illegally across the southern border of the United States every year, generating almost $7 billion annually [36]. According to a joint report by Europol and INTERPOL, 90 percent of the more than 1 million migrants entering the European Union in 2015 used smuggling networks' services. Based on the same report, migrant smugglers made an estimated $5 to $6 billion by smuggling Africans to Europe in 2015 [43].

The trafficking of small arms and light weapons had an estimated market value of US$1.7 billion to $3.5 billion in 2014, which represents

10 to 20 percent of the legal arms trade [37]. The arms trafficking business is growing due to instability in many parts of Africa, South America, and in war-torn countries such as Iraq, Afghanistan, Syria, Libya, and Pakistan.

The trade in counterfeit products and pirated goods is another lucrative crime with an estimated market value of US$923 billion to $1.13 trillion annually [37]. The counterfeit industry includes a wide range of products from books and watches to clothes, food, and pharmaceuticals. Almost 60 to 75 percent of the counterfeit and pirated goods are originated in China. Some counterfeit products such as pharmaceutical drugs and food involve serious health hazards. Due to its intangible nature, the theft of intellectual and cultural properties is very attractive to criminal organizations. The illicit trade of intellectual and cultural properties is estimated at US$1.2 billion to $1.6 billion [37]. Theft of intellectual property includes software, movies, music, video games, trusted brand names, proprietary designs of high-tech devices, and manufacturing processes [38].

Trafficking in natural resources may involve the smuggling of raw materials including timber, wildlife, iron, oil, diamonds, and rare or precious metals. Illegal logging is the most profitable natural resource crime. The value of illegal logging varies between US$52 billion and $157 billion per year. Almost 10 to 30 percent of the world's timber is produced illegally. Southeast Asia, Central Africa, and South America have the highest level of illegal logging and China is the primary destination for the majority of illegally sourced timber [37]. According to a study by the United Nations Environment Program and INTERPOL, the illegal extraction and trade of minerals are estimated between US$12 billion and $48 billion annually [37]. Diamond, gold, and silver are the most illegally mined materials in Africa and South America. Furthermore, the illegal extraction of crude oil was estimated to be worth between US$5.2 billion and US$11.9 billion in 2015. The illegal oil extraction is quite rampant in countries such as Nigeria, Colombia, Indonesia, Mexico, Syria, Russia, and Iraq [37]. The illegal trade in wildlife is estimated between US$5 billion and $23 billion [37]. Elephants, rhinos, pangolins, different types of birds, fish, mammals, and plants are the targets of organized criminals across the world. Similarly, illegal fishing is estimated to generate US$15.5 billion to $36.4 billion annually [37].

Transnational organized crime includes almost all criminal activities motivated by profit. The concentration of illegal wealth and power in the hands of criminal groups is a major challenge to governance at the national and international levels. Moreover, the criminal activities have pernicious implications for public safety, public health, democratic institutions, and economic stability across the globe. Transnational criminal organizations weaken state authority either directly through confrontation or indirectly through corruption. They undermine government monopoly of the use of violence [39]. By accumulating money and power, transnational criminal organizations can threaten democratic institutions and the rule of law, change the elections outcomes, and corrupt institutions. Evidently, many of criminal activities violate human rights, harm the environment, and involve conflicts and loss of life. In some countries with weak institutions, transnational criminal organizations may penetrate the government and cause state authorities facilitate their criminal activities [39]. Considering the substantial accumulated power and wealth of transnational criminal organizations and the global scope of their operations, national responses alone are not suitable to cope with them. Fighting the transnational criminal organizations often requires multilateral and global solutions.

The Maritime Piracy

Maritime piracy is a transnational organized crime because a ship is considered the sovereign territory of the nation whose flag is borne and because it requires significant amounts of planning and expertise [23]. Maritime piracy may involve two offenses: the first is stealing a maritime vessel or its cargo; the second involves kidnapping the vessel and crew until a ransom is paid [24]. Almost 90 percent of the world trade is done via sea routes. Therefore, it is not surprising that, in a globalized economy, maritime piracy is becoming a highly lucrative and a common form of organized crime. In the recent years, piracy has increased due to the growth in the volume of merchandise moving by sea and the desire of transporters to pass through crowded maritime routes [33]. The slack coastal security due to political instability in some war-torn countries, terrorism, and the rise of armed groups are other contributors to the growth of piracy [32]. Facing the rise of piracy, more than 20 countries have formed naval task forces to protect their vessels and enhance the maritime security [34]. The Gulf of Aden near Somalia, the Suez Canal, the Cape of Good Hope, the Persian Gulf, and the Indian Ocean represent some of the most important maritime routes. For instance, almost 33,000 commercial ships travel the Gulf of Aden each year and around 7 percent of the world's maritime commerce passes through the Suez Canal [33]. The terrorist groups may be connected to maritime piracy. It has been reported that al-Shabaab terrorist group is relying on the Somalian pirates to smuggle weapons and jihadist operatives into Somalia [33]. The terrorist networks may use the financial earnings of piracy to fund their activities around the world. In addition to the threat to the maritime security and commercial transit, piracy may have disastrous implications for the environment due to the discharge of oil and other toxic chemicals into the seawater. Despite enhanced security measures, the piracy attacks continue to grow in the horn of Africa and in the Gulf of Aden mainly due to the fragility of Somalian state and the ensuing humanitarian crises. Somalia is engulfed in a devastating combination of conflict, immense displacement, drought, high food prices, and hyperinflation [33]. Furthermore, according to the United Nations Food and Agricultural Organization, foreign ships have taken advantage of the political chaos in Somalia to illegally exploit more than US$450 million of fish stocks off the coast of Somalia, stealing valuable food sources from the Somalian people. Along with illegal fishing, European ships have been dumping toxic and nuclear waste, such as radioactive uranium, hospital waste, and industrial chemicals, in the waters around Somalia [32]. Under these circumstances, maritime piracy can be viewed as an attractive economic activity to the Somalian criminals who may collect up to US$18 to 30 million a year in ransom. In addition to the Gulf of Aden and the greater Indian Ocean, maritime piracy attacks are seen in Southeast Asia and mainly in the Straits of Malacca, through which transit more than 90,000 ships per year, accounting for 40 percent of the world's trade [32]. Likewise, the waters off Nigeria, Tanzania, Bangladesh, and India have seen many maritime piracy predations in the recent years [33]. The direct cost of maritime piracy is estimated between US$1 and 16 billion per year, but the indirect cost and the long-term effects could be even much higher.

References

[1] Bachmann, S.D., and H. Gunneriusson. 2015. "Hybrid Wars: The 21st-Century's New Threats to Global Peace and Security." *Scientia Militaria: South African Journal of Military Studies* 43, no. 1, pp. 77–98.

[2] Chuka, N., and J.F. Born. 2014. *Hybrid Warfare: Implications for CAF Force Development* (No. DRDC-RDDC-2014-R43). Defence Research and Development Canada CORA Ottawa, Ontario Canada.

[3] Hoffman, F.G. 2007. *Conflict in the 21st Century: The Rise of Hybrid Wars,* 51. Arlington: Potomac Institute for Policy Studies.

[4] Metz, S. 2014. "Strategic Horizons: In Ukraine, Russia Reveals Its Mastery of Unrestricted Warfare." *World Politics Review.*

[5] Pomerantsev, P., and M. Weiss. 2014. *The Menace of Unreality: How the Kremlin Weaponizes Information, Culture, and Money.* New York: Institute of Modern Russia.

[6] Glenn, R.W. 2009. "Thoughts on 'Hybrid' Conflict." In *Small Wars Journal* 13. smallwarsjournal.com/mag/docs-temp/188-glenn.pdf (accessed 02.01.2017).

[7] Münkler, H. 2015. "Hybrid Wars. The Dissolution of the Binary Order of War and Peace, and Its Consequences." *Ethics and Armed Forces* 2, pp. 20–23.

[8] Hartman, W.J. 2002. *Globalization and Asymmetrical Warfare* (No. AU/ACSC/053/2001-04). Air Command and Staff Coll Maxwell AFB AL.

[9] Thornton, R. 2007. *Asymmetric Warfare: Threat and Response in the 21st Century.* Polity.

[10] Khalilzad, Z., T. LaTourrette, D.E. Mosher, L.M. Davis, D.R. Howell, and B. Raymond. 1999. *Strategic Appraisal: The Changing Role of Information in Warfare.* Rand Corporation.

[11] National Research Council. 2009. *Technology, Policy, Law, and Ethics Regarding US Acquisition and Use of Cyberattack Capabilities.* National Academies Press.

[12] Billo, C., and W. Chang. 2004. *Cyber Warfare: An Analysis of the Means and Motivations of Selected Nation States.* Dartmouth College, Institute for Security Technology Studies.

[13] Bruce, R., S. Dynes, H. Brechbuhl, B. Brown, E. Goetz, P. Verhoest, E. Luiijf, and S. Helmus. 2005. International Policy Framework for Protecting Critical Information Infrastructure: A Discussion Paper Outlining Key Policy Issues. TNO Report, Tuck School of Business at Dartmouth.

[14] Bajaj, K. 2010. "The Cybersecurity Agenda: Mobilizing for International Action." *EastWest Institute Report,* pp. 81–103.

[15] Harvey, D. 2003. *The New Imperialism.* USA: Oxford University Press.

[16] Cronin, A.K. 2006. "How al-Qaida Ends: The Decline and Demise of Terrorist Groups." *International Security* 31, no. 1, pp. 7–48.

[17] Neumann, P.R., and M.L.R. Smith. 2007. *The Strategy of Terrorism: How It Works, and Why It Fails.* Routledge.

[18] Hoffman, B. 2006. *Inside Terrorism, Revised and Expanded Edition.* New York: Columbia University Press.

[19] Thomson, J.A. 2003. "Killer Apes on American Airlines, or How Religion was the Main Hijacker on September 11." In *Violence or Dialogue: Psychoanalytic Insights on Terror and Terrorism,* eds. S. Varvin and V.D. Volkan. London: International Psychoanalytical Association

[20] Vidino, L. 2006. *Al Qaeda in Europe: The New Battleground of International Jihad.* Prometheus Books.

[21] Ganor, B. 2009. "Trends in Modern International Terrorism." In *To Protect and To Serve,* 11–42. New York: Springer.

[22] Reich, W, ed. 1998. *Origins of Terrorism: Psychologies, Ideologies, Theologies, States of Mind.* Woodrow Wilson Center Press.

[23] Gaibulloev, K., and T. Sandler. 2016. "Decentralization, Institutions, and Maritime Piracy." *Public Choice* 169, nos. 3–4, pp. 357–74.

[24] Marchione, E., and S.D. Johnson. 2013. "Spatial, Temporal and Spatiotemporal Patterns of Maritime Piracy." *Journal of Research in Crime and Delinquency* 50, no. 4, pp. 504–24.

[25] Coker, C. 2014. *Globalisation and Insecurity in the Twenty-first Century: NATO and the Management of Risk.* Routledge.

[26] Biscop, S. 2016. *The European Security Strategy: A Global Agenda for Positive Power.* Routledge.

[27] Saeed, F., M. Rahid, H.Z. Rehman, S. Mobin, and S. Ahmed. 2012. "Tackling Terrorism in Pakistan." *International Journal of Peace and Development Studies* 3, no. 1, pp. 1–5.

[28] Ware, A., and V.A. Ware. 2014. "Development in Fragile States and Situations: Theory and Critique." In *Development in Difficult Sociopolitical Contexts,* 24–47. UK: Palgrave Macmillan.

[29] Rotberg, R.I. 2003. "Failed States, Collapsed States, Weak States: Causes and Indicators." In *State Failure and State Weakness in a Time of Terror,* ed. R.I. Rotberg. Washington, DC: Brookings Institution Press.

[30] Wise, W.M. 2004. "American Perspectives on the Threat Posted by Weak and Failing the Asian States." Paper Presented at the US-China Conference on Areas of Instability and Emerging Threats, Bejing, February 23–24.

[31] Doornbos, M., S. Roque, and S. Woodward. 2006. "Failing States or Failed States? Role of Development Models: Collected works." FRIDE, A European Think Tank for Global Action, February 8; Crocker, C.A. 2003. "Engaging Failed States." *Foreign Affairs* 82, no. 5, September/October.

[32] Chalk, P. Summer 2009. "Sunken Treasures, The Economic Impetus Behind Modern Piracy." *Rand Review*.

[33] Schreier, F. 2015. *On Cyber Warfare*. Geneva, Switzerland: Geneva Centre for the Democratic Control of Armed Forces.

[34] US Naval Forces Central Command, "Combined Task Force 150," http://cusnc.navy.mil/command/ctf150.html; US Navy, "Focus on Combined Task Force 151," http://navy.mil/local/CTF-151

[35] Paoli, L, ed. 2014. *The Oxford Handbook of Organized Crime*. Oxford Handbooks.

[36] UNODC (UN Office on Drugs and Crime). June 17, 2010. *The Globalization of Crime: A Transnational Organized Crime Threat Assessment*. ISBN: 978-92-1-130295-0, available at http://refworld.org/docid/4cad7f892.html (accessed July 15, 2017).

[37] May, C. 2017. "Transnational Crime and the Developing World." Global Financial Integrity. http://creativecommons.org.

[38] Reichel, P., and J. Albanese, eds. 2013. *Handbook of Transnational Crime and Justice*. Sage Publications.

[39] Picarelli, J., and P. Williams. 2000. "Organized Crime and Information Technologies." In *The Information Age Anthology, Part II: National Security Implications of the Information Age*, eds. D. Papp and D.S. Alberts. Washington, DC: NDU Press.

[40] Harvey, D. 1989. *The Condition of Postmodernity*. Oxford: Basil Blackwell.

[41] Giddens, A. 1990. *The Consequence of Modernity*. Cambridge: Polity Press.

[42] Scholte, J.A. 1997. "The Globalisation of World Politics." In *The Globalisation of World Politics: An Introduction*, eds. S. Smith and J. Baylis, 211–44. Oxford: Oxford University Press.

[43] Smugglers made at least $5 billion last year in Europe Migrant (May 17, 2016) Crisis https://nytimes.com/2016/05/18/world/europe/migrants-refugees-smugglers.html?mcubz=1&_r=0

CHAPTER 8

The Giant Corporations

1. An Incredible Concentration of Power and Wealth
2. Doing More with Less: More Revenues and Fewer Employees
3. Stifling Competition: The Winner-Take-All Capitalism
4. Eroding the State Sovereignty and Diluting the Nationhood
5. The Rise of Emerging Markets' Multinationals

An Incredible Concentration of Power and Wealth

For a long time throughout the history, the church and the state have been the political and economic centers of decision making [1]. With the advent of modern capitalism in the 18th century, the corporations gradually outshined the church and the state. For a while, the ability of corporations to grow was restrained by the limits of capital accumulation, geographic location, and legal and cultural barriers, but in the second half of the 19th century, the new regulations allowed the momentous growth of corporations. On the one hand, the concept of limited liability made owners of businesses not subject to punishment for their debts. On the other hand, the financial exchanges facilitated the interaction between investors and businesses and thus allowed the rapid accumulation of capital. The steady growth of corporations continued during the 20th century but gained a remarkable momentum in the 1990s. The end of Cold War, the new information technology, and particularly globalization provided unprecedented drivers for a phenomenal concentration of economic power in a number of large corporations. In 1980, the world's largest 1,000 corporations earned $2.64 trillion in revenue, employed 21 million people, and had a total market capitalization of $900 billion. Thirty years later, in 2012, the world's largest 1,000 corporations made an astonishing $34 trillion in revenue, employed 73 million people, and had a total market capitalization of $28 trillion [1]. Currently, the giant corporations are progressively occupying the skylines of big cities and are accumulating huge amounts of wealth. As of 2015, out of 100 global economies, 69 were corporations whereas only 31 were nations [25] (see Table 8.1).

Table 8.1 *The top 100 largest corporations (2016)*

Corporations versus governments revenues: 2015 data			
Rank	Type	Name	Revenue (US$)
1	Government	The United States	3251000000000
2	Government	China	2426000000000
3	Government	Germany	1515000000000
4	Government	Japan	1439000000000
5	Government	France	1253000000000
6	Government	The United Kingdom	1101000000000
7	Government	Italy	876000000000
8	Government	Brazil	631000000000
9	Government	Canada	585000000000
10	Corporation	Walmart	482130000000
11	Government	Spain	473600000000
12	Government	Australia	425700000000
13	Government	Netherlands	336500000000
14	Corporation	State Grid	329601000000
15	Corporation	China National Petroleum	299271000000
16	Corporation	Sinopec Group	294344000000
17	Government	Korea, South	291300000000
18	Corporation	Royal Dutch Shell	272156000000
19	Government	Mexico	259600000000
20	Government	Sweden	250800000000
21	Corporation	Exxon Mobil	246204000000
22	Corporation	Volkswagen	236600000000
23	Corporation	Toyota Motor	236592000000
24	Government	India	236000000000
25	Corporation	Apple	233715000000
26	Government	Belgium	226800000000
27	Corporation	BP	225982000000
28	Government	Switzerland	221900000000
29	Government	Norway	220200000000
30	Government	Russia	216300000000

31	Corporation	Berkshire Hathaway	210821000000
32	Government	Venezuela	203400000000
33	Government	Saudi Arabia	193000000000
34	Corporation	McKesson	192487000000
35	Government	Austria	189200000000
36	Corporation	Samsung Electronics	177440000000
37	Government	Turkey	175400000000
38	Corporation	Glencore	170497000000
39	Corporation	Industrial & Commercial Bank of China	167227000000
40	Corporation	Daimler	165800000000
41	Government	Denmark	161700000000
42	Corporation	UnitedHealth Group	157107000000
43	Corporation	CVS Health	153290000000
44	Corporation	EXOR Group	152591000000
45	Corporation	General Motors	152356000000
46	Corporation	Ford Motor	149558000000
47	Corporation	China Construction Bank	147910000000
48	Corporation	AT&T	146801000000
49	Corporation	Total	143421000000
50	Government	Argentina	143400000000
51	Corporation	Hon Hai Precision Industry	141213000000
52	Corporation	General Electric	140389000000
53	Corporation	China State Construction Engineering	140159000000
54	Corporation	AmerisourceBergen	135962000000
55	Corporation	Agricultural Bank of China	133419000000
56	Corporation	Verizon	131620000000
57	Government	Finland	131400000000
58	Corporation	Chevron	131118000000
59	Corporation	E.ON	129277000000
60	Corporation	AXA	129250000000
61	Government	Indonesia	123300000000
62	Corporation	Allianz	122948000000
63	Corporation	Bank of China	122337000000
64	Corporation	Honda Motor	121624000000
65	Corporation	Japan Post Holdings	118762000000
66	Corporation	Costco	116199000000

(*Continued*)

Table 8.1 The top 100 largest corporations (2016)

Corporations versus governments revenues: 2015 data			
Rank	Type	Name	Revenue (US$)
67	Corporation	BNP Paribas	111531000000
68	Corporation	Fannie Mae	110359000000
69	Corporation	Ping An Insurance	110308000000
70	Government	The United Arab Emirates	110100000000
71	Corporation	Kroger	109830000000
72	Corporation	Société Générale	107736000000
73	Corporation	Amazon.com	107006000000
74	Corporation	China Mobile Communications	106761000000
75	Corporation	SAIC Motor	106684000000
76	Corporation	Walgreens Boots Alliance	103444000000
77	Corporation	HP	103355000000
78	Corporation	Assicurazioni Generali	102567000000
79	Corporation	Cardinal Health	102531000000
80	Corporation	BMW	102248000000
81	Corporation	Express Scripts Holding	101752000000
82	Corporation	Nissan Motor	101536000000
83	Corporation	China Life Insurance	101274000000
84	Corporation	J.P. Morgan Chase	101006000000
85	Corporation	Gazprom	99464000000
86	Corporation	China Railway Engineering	99435000000
87	Corporation	Petrobras	97314000000
88	Corporation	Trafigura Group	97237000000
89	Corporation	Nippon Telegraph & Telephone	96134000000
90	Corporation	Boeing	96114000000
91	Corporation	China Railway Construction	95652000000
92	Corporation	Microsoft	93580000000
93	Corporation	Bank of America Corp.	93056000000
94	Corporation	ENI	92985000000
95	Corporation	Nestlé	92285000000
96	Corporation	Wells Fargo	90033000000
97	Government	Portugal	89940000000
98	Corporation	HSBC Holdings	89061000000
99	Corporation	Home Depot	88519000000
100	Corporation	Citigroup	88275000000

Source: The Global Justice Now (NGO), CIA World Factbook, and Fortune magazine.

While this method is not an accurate comparison between corporations and nations, it offers a simple impression of the economic influence of large corporations. The world's 10 largest corporations have a combined revenue greater than the government revenue of 180 countries combined including Ireland, Indonesia, Israel, Colombia, Greece, South Africa, Iraq, and Vietnam [12]. Walmart is ranked the 10th economic entity and thus it is considered larger than some major global economies including Australia, South Korea, and India. It is striking to note that the cash that Apple has on hand surpasses the GDPs of almost two-thirds of the world's countries [26]. According to the Fortune Magazine, Walmart, State Grid, China National Petroleum, Sinopec Group, Royal Dutch Shell, Exxon Mobil, Volkswagen, Toyota Motor, Apple, and BP were ranked the largest global corporation in 2015.

Other financial and nonfinancial measures like the number of consumers, market share, and growth rate confirm the extraordinary rise of the giant corporations in the past two decades. For example, Google, Amazon, and Facebook experienced rapid and consistent growth in a matter of 10 to 15 years to become giant corporations. Founded in September 1998, Google processes now over 40,000 search queries every second, over 3.5 billion searches per day, and 1.2 trillion searches per year [27]. Similarly, Facebook that was founded only a decade ago (in 2004) had more than 1.94 billion monthly active users as of March 2017, a number larger than the population of China and the United States together [28]. Amazon.com that started as an online bookseller in 1995 produced net sales of US$136 billion in 2016 [29]. The young tech corporations like Apple, Google, Amazon, and Facebook have become the world's most valuable companies and have reached the astonishing market capitalizations of $737.33 billion, $651.67 billion, $466.15 billion, and $435.27 billion, respectively, as of May 2017.

In the last decade, the global corporations' share of the world's economy has increased drastically while the competition from small and medium-sized businesses has fallen by almost the same factor. As a result, a relatively small number of very large corporations have increased their control over global markets, made higher profits, and effectively outcompeted their smaller rivals. Particularly, the tech giants have capitalized on their vast scales to gain market dominance and produce colossal revenues.

A few companies, six or nine, manage the organization of the information economy from an Internet search, advertising, and electronic retailing to clouding and social media. According to the McKinsey Global Institute, 10 percent of the world's public companies generate almost 80 percent of the profits [2]. The simple rule of thumb is that the larger corporations become more competitive because of their economies of scale, political connections, and huge financial and technological resources. For instance, those corporations with more than $1 billion in the annual revenue account for 60 percent of total global revenues [2]. The concentration of wealth in the giant corporations is particularly impressive in the United States where the share of GDP generated by the Fortune 100 biggest American companies surged from about 33 percent of GDP in 1994 to 46 percent in 2013 [2]. Some of these giant corporations such as ExxonMobil, Berkshire Hathaway, Procter & Gamble, Wal-Mart Stores, Pfizer, and Johnson & Johnson have had established themselves many decades ago. Some others like Apple, Alphabet, Microsoft, Amazon.com, and Facebook are tech companies that have joined the club of giant corporations more recently. While most of these giant corporations are originated in the United States, Western Europe, and Japan, some others like Alibaba, ICBC, and China Mobile belong to the emerging countries.

Doing More with Less: More Revenues and Fewer Employees

Traditionally, the firms' revenues, market capitalizations, and assets were correlated to the number of employees. In other words, those firms that had big revenues also typically had large workforces and substantial assets, as well as large market capitalizations. In the past three decades, with the advent of globalization and new information technologies, the large multinational corporations are doing more with less, meaning that they are generating more revenues with fewer employees and less physical assets [3]. Nowadays, the corporations can be small in assets and employees, but big in revenues and profits (Table 8.2). This feature may be found particularly in high-technology sectors that offer intangible services. Facebook with only 17,000 employees in 2016 generated revenues of $27.638 billion and had a market capitalization of $342 billion. Netflix

Table 8.2 The top 50 companies ranked by revenue per employee in 2016

S & P 500 Companies with Highest Revenue Per Employee

Top 50 companies ranked by revenue per employee (2016)

Rank	Company	RPE	Sector
1	Amerisource Bergen	$7.9 M	Healthcare
2	Valero Energy Corporation	$7.6 M	Energy
3	Phillips 66	$5.7 M	Energy
4	Express Scripts Holding Company	$3.9 M	Healthcare
5	Tesoro Corporation	$3.9 M	Energy
6	ONEOK	$3.7 M	Energy
7	Gilead Sciences	$3.4 M	Healthcare
8	Cardinal Health	$3.3 M	Healthcare
9	Exxon Mobil Corporation	$3.2 M	Energy
10	Altria Group	$3.1 M	CS*
11	EOG Resources	$2.9 M	Energy
12	Mckesson	$2.8 M	Healthcare
13	Devon Energy Corporation	$2.4 M	Energy
14	Chesapeake Energy Corporation	$2.4 M	Energy
15	Reynolds American	$2.3 M	CS*
16	Lyondell Basell Industries	$2.2 M	Materials
17	Aflac	$2.2 M	Financials
18	Chevron Corporation	$2.2 M	Energy
19	Marathon Oil	$2.2 M	Energy
20	Hess Corporation	$2.1 M	Energy
21	Cabot Oil & Gas Corporation	$2.0 M	Energy
22	Archer Daniels Midland Company	$2.0 M	CS*
23	Netfix	$1.9 M	CD*
24	Apple	$1.9 M	IT*
25	Conoco Phillips	$1.8 M	Energy
26	Anadarko Petroleum Corporation	$1.7 M	Energy
27	D.R. Horton	$1.7 M	CD*
28	Facebook	$1.6 M	IT*
29	PulteGroup	$1.6 M	CD*
30	Anthem	$1.6 M	Healthcare
31	Celgene Corporation	$1.6M	Healthcare

(Continued)

Table 8.2 (Continued)

Rank	Company	RPE	Sector
32	Biogen	$1.5 M	Healthcare
33	Noble Energy	$1.5 M	Energy
34	Concho Resources	$1.5 M	Energy
35	Newfiled Exploration	$1.5 M	Energy
36	Lincoln National Corporation	$1.5 M	Financials
37	Cimarex Energy	$1.5 M	Energy
38	Murphy Oil Corporation	$1.4 M	Energy
39	Range Resources Corporation	$1.4 M	Energy
40	Apache Corporation	$1.4 M	Energy
41	Marathon Petroleum Corporation	$1.4 M	Energy
42	XL Group	$1.4 M	Financials
43	NRG Energy	$1.4 M	Utilities
44	Viacom	$1.3 M	CD*
45	Williams Companies	$1.3 M	Energy
46	CME Group	$1.3 M	Financials
47	Centene Corp	$1.3 M	Healthcare
48	Lennar Corporation	$1.3 M	CD*
49	Aetna	$1.3 M	Healthcare
50	Twenty-First Century Fox	$1.3 M	CD*

*CD - Consumer Discretionary, CS - Consumer Staples, IT - Information Technology

Source: businessinsider.com

with a market capitalization of over $51 billion and revenues of almost $8.83 billion had only 3,500 employees in 2015. The examples of firms with large revenues and huge market valuations but very small workforce and insignificant tangible assets are not limited to information technology. In the recent years, automation, global production, and outsourcing have enabled the giant corporations to enhance their productivity and generate more revenues with fewer employees and fewer assets. Nike, Apple, Vizio, Exxon Mobil, and AT&T are other examples of those firms that have increased their productivity by cutting their workforce. Exxon Mobil, the world's most successful oil company, has reduced its workforce from 150,000 in the 1960s to less than 75,000, despite having merged with a giant rival [2]. Those firms that have not been able to reduce the number of their personnel tend to hire low-wage workers that ultimately do not cost them very much. It is interesting to note that large corporations employ a grand majority (66 percent) of low-wage workers in America [4]. The American large corporations have mostly recovered from the recession of 2007 to 2008 and are generally in strong financial positions. They are currently generating more revenues as a percentage of the economy, but wages as a percentage of the economy are at an all-time low. Walmart, which is the largest American employer with more than 1.5 million employees, has one of the lowest wages in the United States estimated at $12.94 per hour. Other retailers such as Kroger (400,000 employees), Home Depot (371,000 employees), and Target (347,000 employees) are among top employers. Some fast-food chains including McDonald's and YUM Brands have larger employment rolls but rely heavily on part-time and temporary workers. In other words, top employers in the United States are mainly in retail and fast-food industries where employees face low wages, high turnover, minimal benefits, and low career opportunities. Other giant corporations are increasingly relying on a more flexible organizational structure such as labor on-demand model. More recently, Uber and Airbnb have developed business models that are able to generate colossal revenues independent of their workforce. Based on these observations, it is possible to suggest that rising corporate profits come to the detriment of the American workers [30]. The giant corporations visibly favor shareholders' returns over employees' interests and consider the reduction in their workforce as an important step toward profit maximization.

Stifling Competition: The Winner-Take-All Capitalism

The giant corporations are benefitting from their immense financial, technological, and managerial resources, to develop sophisticated competitive advantages against smaller rivals. In the technology sector, a few corporations like Google, Microsoft, Facebook, and Amazon have become so dominant that practically are stifling the competition from the small and even mid-sized companies [2]. Likewise, in the financial sector, five large banks control 45 percent of American banking assets. The 10 biggest banks control almost 50 percent of assets under management worldwide [26]. The wave of consolidation has swept all the U.S. industries from aviation and telecommunication to insurance, pharmaceutical, news, and media. While the phenomenon of consolidation is particularly striking in the United States, European and Asian countries follow almost the same trajectory. Capitalizing on the global logistics and production, large corporations can conveniently scatter their supply chains across the world and take advantage of local endowments. The global presence especially is advantageous to those digital and knowledge-based companies that rely on a lean workforce and intangible assets to generate significant revenues [2]. In order to overcome the tax codes, the giant corporations often get involved in complex financial engineering and keep their revenues or assets in low-tax countries. According to the United Nations Conference on Trade and Development (UNCTAD), the top 100 largest corporations have an average of 20 holding firms each and more than 500 affiliates that are often domiciled in low-tax jurisdictions [2]. Apple, an American giant that is based in California, set up two bogus companies with no employees in Ireland to avoid significant tax bills in the United States in 2015. According to the Financial Times [31], about 90 percent of Apple's foreign profits were reported by Irish subsidiaries, which were highly profitable, but paid little tax because they were not tax-resident anywhere. It is estimated that Apple paid 0.005 percent tax on its European profits in 2014 [13]. As the environment of business is becoming more complex and more regulated, the larger corporations have the luxury of mobilizing the armies of their experienced administrators and consultants to benefit from the legal loopholes, lacunas, and ambiguities at the expense of smaller firms. The result is obvious: The large corporations dodge taxes, but the small and medium-sized firms have to pay a hefty price.

The very large corporations are increasingly connected to cronyism. They are using their power to maximize their profits unethically and even illegally. General Electric, Boeing Co, Northrop Grumman, Comcast Corporation, Verizon Communications, FedEx Corporation, Exxon Mobil, Lockheed Martin, Pfizer, Amazon.com, Facebook, and Google are on the top of the list in lobbying expenditures [14]. According to Oxfam-documented reports, more than 140 corporations from all sectors including finance, extractives, garment, defense, energy, technology, and pharmaceutical are using their influence to establish political connections to shape national and international policies [15]. In the United

States, large corporations spend about $2.6 billion a year on lobbying expenditures. Furthermore, the large multinationals often hire former government officials as their senior managers or members of the board of directors to push their strategic agendas. In addition to keeping a good number of their own lobbyists on Capitol Hill, some firms use professional lobbyists to apply a constant pressure on lawmakers. They know that investment in lobbying is paying good dividends as the federal government extends its power over sensitive areas such as health care, technology, telecommunication, and financial markets [2]. The phenomenon of business lobbying is not limited to American corporations. The centers of political decision making in the European Union are flooded with a large number of professional lobbyists who are advancing the corporate causes. For instance, Brussels is home to at least 30,000 business lobbyists who try to influence legislation and regulation for more than 500 million European customers [2]. Some of these professional and well-paid corporate lobbyists are former politicians or government officials who are very knowledgeable about the intricacies of the legislature. While the very large corporations receive special treatments from the governments and lawmakers, the small and midsized businesses struggle to abide by complex rules.

The giant corporations are able to effectively transfer and manage their resources across national borders. They benefit from savings in low-cost countries through outsourcing contracts that do not require large capital investments. Indeed, they can, depending on the markets' conditions, quickly modify or cancel their contracts. By relying on the outsourcing contracts, they are able to evade the responsibility for establishing fair labor practices and meeting environmental standards [5]. In other words, the large multinational corporations are so powerful that they can create a global job competition across the world, granting shares of production only to those nations who offer them the highest concessions and the lowest demands [6]. Tax breaks, human rights abuses, child labor, and lax environmental standards are some examples of concessions that the host nations offer to the giant multinationals. For instance, Malaysia attracted manufacturing operations from some semiconductor multinationals by offering them tax breaks on earnings and preventing the workers from forming unions [5].

In the past two decades, the large corporations have earned huge efficiencies by scattering their value chain activities across the world, forming strategic partnership and alliances, and capitalizing on the economies of scale. It is estimated that the top 1,000 public American companies generate about 40 percent of their revenues from alliances and acquisitions [15]. The large corporations are able to accumulate huge amounts of cash that allow them to acquire smaller firms, develop new products, innovate, and wage price wars. For example, Apple's enormous cash reserves in 2016 first quarter were estimated at $246.09 billion. Thanks to such massive financial resources, the giant corporations can effectively absorb the market downturn and survive economic and political crises. Acquiring smaller firms is an effective strategy allowing the acquirer to benefit from the existing technologies, processes, and market shares. Facebook acquired Instagram in 2012 and WhatsApp in 2014, respectively, for $1 and $22 billion to capitalize on their existing platforms. In order to benefit from Indian low-cost and abundant talents, General Electric develops a significant portion of new health care products in India [2]. Thanks to their huge financial and managerial resources, the large multinationals can successfully exploit the cross-national differences with regard to research and development, operations, logistics, and innovation. The large corporations have become so powerful that they are almost killing any competition from other firms even the midsized businesses. In the past decades, we have witnessed the demise of Nokia, Motorola, and Blackberry as a direct result of competitive pressure from Apple Inc. According to McKinsey the average company's tenure on the S&P 500 list has fallen from 61 years in 1958 to 18 years in 2011, implying that, due to competitive pressure, a relatively big number of companies are disappearing [2].

Eroding the State Sovereignty and Diluting the Nationhood

The very large corporations take advantage of the international system on the one hand and influence nations' policies on the other hand. Nations need the multinational corporations in order to attract FDI, create jobs, and boost economic growth and development. The presence of multinational corporations can lead to increased tax revenues that allow the governments to pursue their political programs. Large multinational corporations can dictate to their host countries what they want. They do not need to use corrupt, illegal or even unethical practices to influence the local governments in order to attain their objectives. If a state, especially an economically ailing one, decides to rescind a large corporation permit, the corporation has the option to transfer its assets and investments to another country and deprive the state of its investments and operations [7]. This will result in harm to the state's economy rather than to the corporation's interests. Large global corporations have many features that put them at advantage vis-à-vis nation-states. For instance, corporations are mobile and are driven by purely economic interests that, due to globalization and advances in technology, are not impeded by territorial and cultural boundaries [8]. Once the large multinational corporations obtain access to a country, they become active players not only in the domestic economic sector but also in the political, social, and cultural spheres of the host country. Due to their economic influence, the large multinational corporations can lawfully lobby governments to change policies and legislation with the aim of increasing profits. Furthermore, corporations may engage directly in social activities to set standards for providing public services such as health care and education. The large corporations may put pressure on smaller states, manipulate them, or even plunder their resources in the name of the business, profits maximization, or charity [9].

Because of their influence, the large multinationals have become an increasing threat to states' sovereignty. They have brought about the fragmentation of political authority. They have blurred the boundary between politics, law, and regulation on the one hand and the market and economic activities on the other hand [10]. While the states remain the most important actors, the large corporations are overshadowing their political power in the new international system. Therefore, we may suggest that, due to effects of large corporations, the capacity of states is diminishing in providing public goods and services such as guarding the property rights, maintaining a stable currency system, enforcing contracts, and protecting the natural environment [11].

In the 1950s, General Motors President Charles Wilson famously said, "What was good for our country was good for General Motors and vice versa" [26]. Currently, the interests of corporations and their home countries are separate and to some extent conflicting. The large corporations such as Apple, Walmart, Amazon.com, Unilever, and Black-Rock choose locations for their personnel and operations on the basis of their shareholders' interests, not on the basis of national interests. Some of the largest American corporations including Apple, IBM, Microsoft, and General Electric are exporting jobs to other countries and are hoarding billions of dollars in tax-free or low-tax jurisdictions. Accordingly, national interests are not always prioritized, rather they are often neglected. The world is entering an era in which the most powerful law is not that of national sovereignty but that of profit maximization. By prioritizing their shareholders' interests and by extending their operations beyond national jurisdictions, the large corporations are diluting the very concept of nationhood.

The Rise of Emerging Markets' Multinationals

An important trend in the contemporary world is the rise of emerging markets' multinationals [16, 17]. China Mobile and Lenovo of China, Embraer and Metalúrgica Gerdau of Brazil, Samsung and LG of South Korea, Reliance Industries and Tata of India, and Lukoil and Gazprom of Russia are becoming symbols of a new breed of multinational companies originated in emerging countries. They are expanding rapidly and leaving a permanent mark on global markets. The number of emerging markets' multinationals in the Fortune Global 500 list of the world's biggest companies is going up progressively. The emerging markets' multinationals are aggressively trying to catch up with their counterparts in developed economies and are making their presence felt in the global marketplace [17, 18]. According to the United Nations World Investment Report, in 2010 there were approximately 21,500 multinationals based in emerging markets [16]. Among the top Fortune Global 500 multinationals, there were 95 companies from developing countries in 2010, compared to only 19 in 1990. According to McKinsey, by 2025 some 45 percent of the Fortune Global 500 will be based in emerging economies [2]. Currently, the emerging markets' corporations account for over 40 percent of world exports and around a quarter of outward FDI flows [18].

Central to the rise of emerging markets' multinationals was the increased economic liberalization that happened across the world in the past three decades. The economic liberalization in China started with Deng Xiaoping's reforms in 1978. In India, it led to bureaucratic and economic reforms in the early 1990s and, as a result, reduced governmental intervention in the private sector [19]. In Europe, it was marked by the fall of Berlin Wall in 1989 and the subsequent collapse of the Soviet Union in 1991. The end of centrally planned economies in the Eastern Europe in the 1990s and the advent of neoliberal policies in Latin America and North America intensified further economic liberalization and stimulated market forces across the world, thus creating the right conditions for private businesses to enter global markets [20, 21]. At the same time, the relationships among world businesses were deepened by the formation and expansion of regional blocs such as the European Union, NAFTA, ASEAN, and MERCOSUR. Because of the increased openness, companies and individuals gained access to overseas talent, technology, capital, and management practices. Large trade surpluses, high savings rates, and more importantly, less restrictive monetary policies strengthened the rising levels of liquidity and improved financing conditions for emerging markets' multinationals. At the same time, privatization created an "ethos of entrepreneurship," introduced the profit motive to business transactions, and encouraged a healthy desire for excellence and global competitiveness in developing economies. Many developing countries such as China, India, Brazil, and Russia suddenly allowed the accumulation of personal wealth and capital gains from business activities. Additionally, they took measures to promote outward FDI. For example, the Chinese government aggressively promoted the outward expansion of its firms in order to increase the competitiveness of its industries [21].

The most visible characteristic of emerging markets' multinationals is the accelerated pace of their expansion [22]. According to the *Financial Times'* Global 500 List, the number of multinationals from Brazil, China, India, and Russia quadrupled from 15 to 62 in two years between 2006 and 2008. Thanks to organizational flexibility and innovation, emerging markets' multinationals are capable of competing with the well-established multinationals from advanced countries. For that reason, they often get rid of conventional organizational structures and instead implement flexible, global, and decentralized organizational configurations [22].

Many emerging markets' multinationals are directly supported by their central governments, enjoy strong political connections, and as a result have a political advantage over their Western counterparts. These political capabilities coupled with the high growth rates of their respective countries provide them with the required resources to expand into foreign countries [23]. The emerging markets' multinationals often expand globally, upgrade their capabilities in parallel, and usually enter developed and developing markets simultaneously. Emerging markets' multinationals are not big innovators; rather they are often imitators that copy intellectual property from their rivals in advanced economies. More recently, some emerging markets' multinationals are showing a move toward innovation and creativity [24]. The examples of innovators include Mahindra and Mahindra's Scorpio of India, Embraer of Brazil, and Sasol of South Africa. It seems that emerging markets multinationals' innovation is based on developing countries' needs, constraints, cultural values, and customs. For instance, much of Haier's success is attributed to developing products adapted to Chinese customers.

The emerging markets' multinationals from Russia, South Africa, and Brazil have taken advantage of their countries' vast natural resources and those from China and India have capitalized on their large home markets and the availability of low-cost skilled and unskilled labor. Many Chinese multinational corporations were created as state-owned enterprises and are still receiving considerable backing from the central government including privileged loans, incentives, technology, and favorable tax regimes. Emerging markets' multinationals have excellent capabilities in adapting new technologies and processes to developing countries' contexts. Ironically, the condition of being a latecomer in global markets might represent an advantage for firms engaging in international activities. In comparison with their Western counterparts, emerging markets' multinationals have a superior capacity to understand consumers' needs and preferences in developing countries, and therefore are able to target them more effectively. They are sensitive to variations in consumer habits caused by differences in culture and geography and swiftly adapt to local market requirements. For instance, the Chinese firms added features not found in Western products to respond to the customers' needs in rural

China. Thanks to their sociocultural proximity with developing countries, emerging markets' multinationals also have the ability to manage uncertain, volatile, and even harsh business conditions of emerging markets. The examples include dealing with weak infrastructure, poor road conditions, health or security hazards, vague government policies, and erratic financial markets.

References

[1] Serafeim, G. 2013. The Role of the Corporation in Society: An Alternative View and Opportunities for Future Research.

[2] The Economist 2016. The Rise of the Superstars, Special Report, September 17th, 2016.

[3] Davis, J. 2015. "Capital Markets and Job Creation in the 21st Century." *The Brookings Institution.* www.Brookings.edu/~/media/research/files/papers/2015/12/30-21st-century-job-creationdavis/capital_markets.pdf

[4] National Employment Law Project 2012. Big Business, Corporate Profits, and the Minimum Wage, Data Brief.

[5] Roach, B. 2007. *Corporate Power in a Global Economy.* Medford, MA: Global Development and Environment Institute, Tufts University.

[6] Greider, W. 1998. *One World, Ready or Not: The Manic Logic of Global Capitalism.* Simon and Schuster.

[7] Baylis, J., P. Owens, and S. Smith. (Eds.). 2017. *The Globalization of World Politics: An Introduction to International Relations.* Oxford University Press.

[8] Detomasi, D. 2015. "The Multinational Corporation as a Political Actor: 'Varieties of Capitalism' Revisited." *Journal of Business Ethics* 128, no. 3, pp. 685–700.

[9] Sassen, S. 2015. *Losing Control?: Sovereignty in the Age of Globalization.* Columbia University Press.

[10] Kobrin, S.J. 2008. "12 Globalization, Transnational Corporations and the Future of Global Governance." *Handbook of Research on Global Corporate Citizenship.*

[11] Cerny, P.G. 1995. "Globalization and the Changing Logic of Collective Action." *International Organization* 49, no. 4, pp. 595–625.

[12] Hardoon, D., R. Fuentes-Nieva, and S. Ayele. 2016. An Economy For the 1%: How Privilege and Power in the Economy Drive Extreme Inequality and How this can be Stopped.

[13] Browning, L., and D. Kocieniewski. September 1, 2016. "Pinning Down Apple's Alleged 0.005% Tax Rate Is Nearly Impossible." Bloomberg Technology (website). https://bloomberg.com/news/articles/2016-09-01/pinning-down-apple-s-alleged-0-005-tax-rate-mission-impossible

[14] Wheelwright, G. September 25, 2016. "What are the Big Tech Companies Lobbying for this Election?." The Guardian website. https://theguardian.com/technology/2016/sep/26/tech-news-lobby-election-taxes-tpp-national-security

[15] Allison, C., E. Fleisje, W. Glevey, and W.L. Johannes. 2014. *Trends and Key Drivers of Income Inequality.* Marshall Economic Research Group, University of Cambridge

[16] Berrill, J., and G. Mannella. 2013. "Are Firms from Developed Markets more International than Firms from Emerging Markets?." *Research in International Business and Finance* 27, no. 1, pp. 147–61.

[17] Goldstein, A., and P. Pananond. 2008. "New Multinationals from Singapore and Thailand: The Political Economy of Regional Expansion." In *New Dimensions of Economic Globalization, World Scientific,* eds. R. Rajan, R. Kumar e N. Virgill (a cura di), 209–49.

[18] Lorenzen, M., and R. Mudambi. 2012. "Clusters, Connectivity and Catch-up: Bollywood and Bangalore in the Global Economy." *Journal of Economic Geography* 13, no. 3, pp. 501–34.

[19] Stucchi, T., T. Pedersen, and V. Kumar. 2015. "The Effect of Institutional Evolution on Indian firms' Internationalization: Disentangling Inward-and Outward-Oriented Effects." *Long Range Planning* 48, no. 5, pp. 346–59.

[20] Chen, P.L., and D. Tan. 2016, "Foreign Knowledge Acquisition Through Inter-Firm Collaboration and Recruitment: Implications for the Domestic Growth of Emerging Market Firms." *International Business Review* 25, no. 1, pp. 221–32.

[21] Gaffney, N., D. Cooper, B. Kedia, and J. Clampit. 2014. "Institutional Transitions, Global Mindset, and EMNE Internationalization." *European Management Journal* 32, no. 3, pp. 383–91.

[22] Guillén, M.F., and E. García-Canal. 2009. "The American Model of the Multinational Firm and the New Multinationals from Emerging Economies." *The Academy of Management Perspectives* 23, no. 2, pp. 23–35.

[23] Cuervo-Cazurra, A., and R. Ramamurti. (Eds.). 2014. *Understanding Multinationals from Emerging Markets.* Cambridge, MA: Cambridge University Press.

[24] Immelt, J.R., V. Govindarajan, and C. Trimble. 2009. "How GE is Disrupting Itself." *Harvard Business Review* 87, no. 10, pp. 56–65.

[25] https://weforum.org/agenda/2016/10/corporations-not-countries-dominate-the-list-of-the-world-s-biggest-economic-entities/

[26] Khanna, P., & Rodriguez, I. B. E. (2016). These 25 Companies Are More Powerful Than Many Countries. *Foreign Policy, March/April.*

[27] http://internetlivestats.com/google-search-statistics/

[28] https://zephoria.com/top-15-valuable-facebook-statistics/

[29] https://statista.com/topics/846/amazon/

[30] http://nationalreview.com/article/388780/myth-corporate-profits-matt-palumbo

[31] https://ft.com/content/3e0172a0-6e1b-11e6-9ac1-1055824ca907

CHAPTER 9

The Inequality, the Wealth Concentration, and the Super-Rich

1. The Rise of Economic Inequality in America
2. The Economic Inequality across the World
3. The Causes of Inequality
4. The Consequences of Inequality
5. The Plutocrats or the Global Super-Rich
6. The Popular Myths About Wealth and Poverty

The Rise of Economic Inequality in America

For most of the 20th century, inequality in the United States was flat or falling [1]. After the Second World War between 1947 and the early 1970s, all income groups, particularly the poor, benefited from the national economic growth and experienced growth in real annual income [3]. During this period, government policies were linking productivity to workers' compensation, full employment was a priority, unions were strong, and fiscal policies were equitable [3]. As a result, for much of the period between the1950s and 1970s, inequality was either stable or declining. Things changed since the late 1970s when economic inequality started to rise rapidly. During the past four decades, the economic inequality has constantly risen and currently, it has reached to the levels not seen since the late 1920s [9, 4, 5, 6]. The share of American top 1 percent from the national income jumped from 8 percent in 1979 to more than 18 percent in 2007 meaning an increase of 125 percent. If we include income from capital gains in the calculation, the share of the top 1 percent of the national income reaches over 23 percent, implying a much sharper increase in the economic inequality [2]. Between 2000 and 2008 when George W. Bush was in the White House, productivity grew faster than ever, but the real compensation of all Americans except the top 20 percent was either flat or declining [3]. In other words, gains in wages benefited mostly the rich. In fact, over the last 30 years, the growth in the incomes of the bottom 50 percent has been zero, but incomes of the top 1 percent have grown almost 300 percent [25]. The top 1 percent of Americans control one-third of the assets in the United States. According to Forbes magazine, 492 billionaires in America own more than $2 trillion in different types of assets [52]. The median family income in the United States has been stagnant for over two decades. While the rich get richer, the poor are getting even poorer. What is more, this growing economic disparity is happening despite greater productivity per worker in all sectors [10]. The rich have distanced not only from the poor but also from the rest of society including the middle-class citizens. It is interesting to note that the United States is the most unequal member of developed countries. The data collected from OECD, a club of mainly rich countries, show that the United States is marked by the third-highest level of inequality. What is even more striking is that the U.S. tax system does little to mitigate the economic inequality [7, 11]. For example, tax rates on top incomes have continued to fall in the recent years. The top rate of income tax was 70 percent in 1980, but it is now 40 percent [30]. The rich not only accumulate wealth, but also hand over some colossal assets to their heirs, and thus make the economic inequality even worse. Another trend in economic inequality is the widening gap between the privileged professionals, managers, and business owners and the regular white-collar and blue-collar employees [15] (see Figures 9.1, 9.2, 9.3, and 9.4).

The signs of widening economic inequality and the associated socioeconomic segregation can be seen everywhere across the nation from cities and neighborhoods to public schools, colleges, and hospitals. It is estimated that about 50 percent of retirees will run short of their planned financial needs and might have to continue to work after their 60s [9]. The number of bankruptcies, mortgage foreclosures, and car repossessions skyrocketed between 1970 and 2001 [8]. Job loss, medical expenses, and divorce have been reported as the main factors that push the middle-class

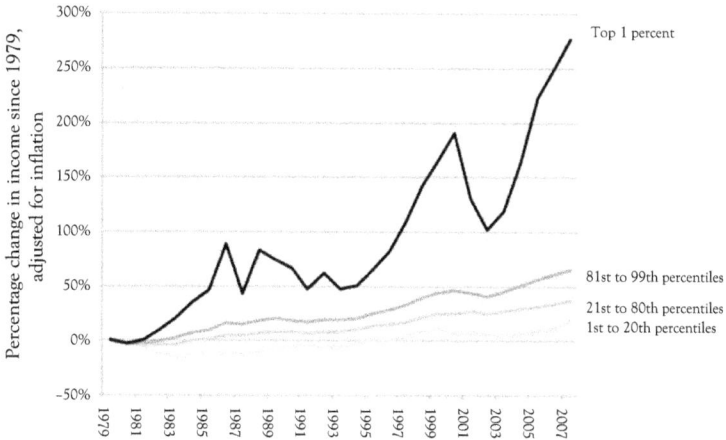

Figure 9.1 A historical overview of the distribution of household income in the United States

Source: Congressional budget office I Graphic: Hagit Bachrach

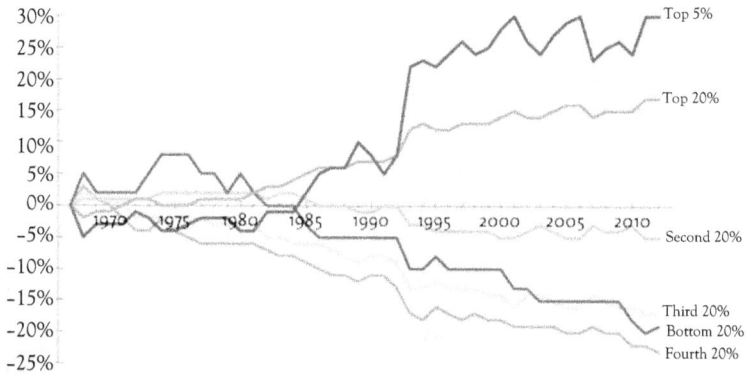

Figure 9.2 A historical overview of the change in share of total income in the United States between 1967 and 2012

Source: Census Bureau

citizens to file for bankruptcy [7]. Most of the middle-class Americans have insufficient savings or are highly indebted. Compared to the early 1970s, Americans spend 21 percent less on clothing, 22 percent less on food, and 44 percent less on major appliances [9]. Many families are hardly staying afloat with two parents working [13]. They live paycheck to paycheck.

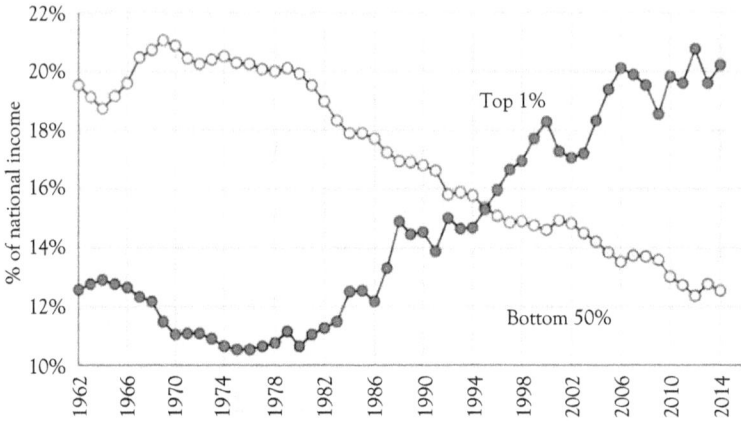

Figure 9.3 Pretax national income shares of the top 1% and the bottom 50% between 1962 and 2014

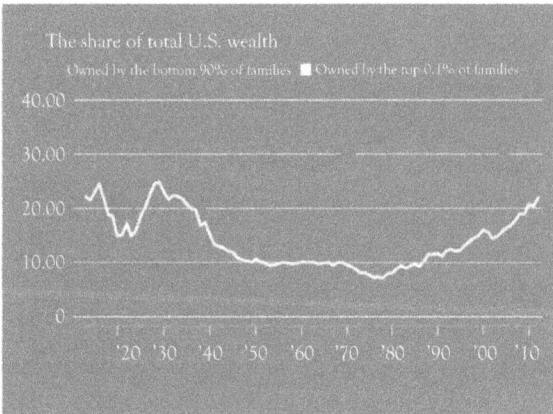

Figure 9.4 The share of total U.S. wealth owned by the top 0.1% and the bottom 90% in the past 100 years

Source: http://gabriel-zucman.eu/files/uswealth/AppendixTables(Aggregates).xlsx

Based on a recent survey conducted by the Federal Reserve Board, almost half of Americans would have trouble finding as little as $400 to pay for an emergency [18]. The United States as the richest country in the world has the highest rates of poverty among the developed nations mainly due to the public and fiscal policies. The poverty rates of American children are on average three or four times greater than in other developed countries [16]. According to the Federal Reserve surveys, the percentage of household disposable income spent on debt services including mortgage, auto loan, and credit card debt has constantly risen in the past 30 years [9]. The average household owes about $176,000 including $29,000 in auto loans and $17,000 in credit card debt. Furthermore, 44 million Americans are burdened by student loan debt. As of 2016, the total of student loan is estimated over $1.3 trillion implying that the average American graduate has $37,000 in student loan debt. To put things in perspective, it is important to mention that the median household income in the United States has fallen from $67,673 in 1999 to $62,462 in 2014, suggesting that the minimum income needed to be a middle-income household fell from $45,115 in 1999 to $41,641 in 2014 [17]. At the same time, the share of American adults in middle-income households has fallen from 55 percent in 2000 to 51 percent in 2014 [17]. The most conspicuous form of economic inequality is seen along the racial lines. Minorities including African Americans, Hispanics, and women who head families are particularly feeling the financial pressure. The typical white household possesses 12-fold more wealth than the average black household does. More than 61 percent of black and 50 percent of Hispanic households do not possess any type of financial asset, compared with 25 percent of their white households [15].

The Economic Inequality Across the World

The global distribution of wealth both among and within nations is highly skewed. According to the World Bank, those nations with gross national income (GNI) per capita of $12,476 or more are categorized as high income while those with a GNI per capita of $1,025 or less are classified as low-income countries [19]. High-income countries constitute 16 percent of the world's population but produce almost 55 percent of global income [19]. By contrast, low-income countries that account for 72 percent of the world's population generate around 1 percent of global income. Most of the high-income countries are located in North America, the Western Europe, or East Asia. The very poor countries are located mostly in the Sub-Saharan Africa and Asia. Due to high economic growth in China in the past three decades, hundreds of millions of Chinese people have been lifted out of poverty [25]. If China is excluded from calculations, it is found that international income inequality has increased significantly between 1980 and 2000 for most of the world's countries. During this period, Latin America, Sub-Saharan Africa, and most parts of the Eastern Europe experienced sharp drops in the level of their gross national income per capita. Between 2000 and 2010, the income inequality between the poor and rich countries has been falling mainly because of the fast economic growth across the world and particularly in the low-income nations. Nevertheless, the absolute income gap between the rich and the poor countries has increased from $18,525 in 1980 to close to $32,900 in 2007 [19].

At the individual level, the world is marked by a striking level of economic inequality where 1 percent of humanity controls as much wealth as the bottom 99 percent [32]. According to Credit Suisse, the poorest 50 percent of the world's population collectively have less than a quarter of 1 percent of the global wealth [26]. This outrageous concentration of wealth is part of a long-term trend that is constantly aggravating. In the past four decades, the economic inequality within nations has been growing faster almost everywhere in the world. For instance, between 1988 and 2011 the income of the poorest 10 percent of people increased by less than $3 a year whereas the income of the richest 1 percent surged 182 times [27]. The growing inequality within nations is not limited to the United States. In the United Kingdom, France, China, and India economic inequality levels are at all-time high. In China, the top 10 percent of the population earns almost 60 percent of the income. South Africa is becoming one of the most unequal countries, even more, unequal than it used to be at the end of apartheid [42]. Across the world, the incomes of the top 1 percent have increased 60 percent in 20 years and the great financial crisis of 2007 has made the rich even richer [37]. In the years after the Great Recession (2007, 2008), the luxury goods market has shown a strong growth across the globe, indicating the growing purchasing power of the rich (Figures 9.5 and 9.6)

To figure out the level of economic inequality in the world, it is interesting to note that only "eight individuals" own the same amount of wealth as the poorest half of the world [28]. A typical chief executive officer of an FTSE-100 company could earn as much in a year as 10,000 Bangladeshi workers [29]. In Vietnam, the rich could earn more in a day than the poor persons earn in 10 years [20]. What is particularly disturbing about the distribution of wealth is that the children, the youth, and

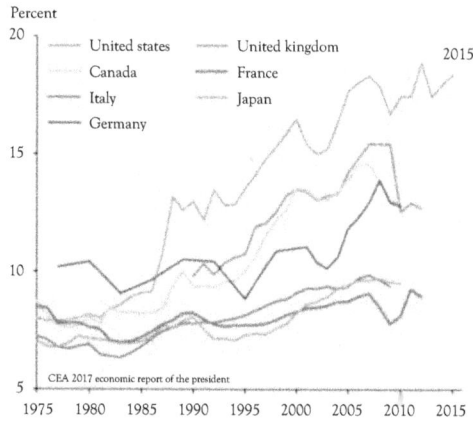

Figure 9.5 Share of income earned by the top 1% in seven advanced economies

Source: World wealth and income database.

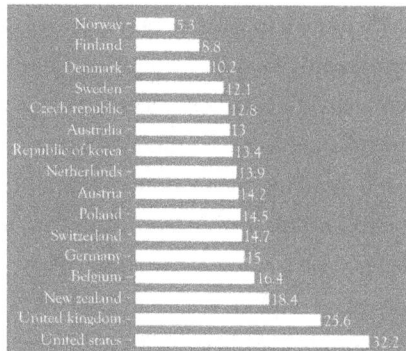

Figure 9.6 A comparison of child poverty rate among advanced economies

Source: http://www.unicef.irc.org/publications/pdf/rc12-eng-web.pdf

the women often fall in the poorest income quintiles. Due to an abject level of poverty, a large number of women and children are exploited by multinationals and are forced to work under inhumane working conditions. For instance, the lowest-paid workers in the garment industry in Asia are mostly women and girls [30].

Many empirical analyses confirm that in the past three decades, economic inequality has increased in most of the societies across the world particularly in all transitional and postcommunist societies [44]. The majority of developed countries experienced rising levels of inequality since the 1970s [45]. Currently, economic inequality is higher than during the 1980s, and it is substantially sharper in the developing than in the developed world [45]. Relying on the Gini index, we find that Eastern European and the former Soviet countries have experienced the highest levels of economic inequality between 1990 and 2008. Moreover, across the world, the middle-income countries are marked by the highest levels of economic inequality. Despite some recent improvements, Latin America is categorized as the region with the highest level of income inequality. The patterns of inequality vary across Africa, but Sub-Saharan Africa is recognized as extremely unequal [46].

The Causes of Inequality

The deepening economic inequality in the United States and across the world can be attributed to a wide range of political, fiscal, technological, and demographic factors. In the past three decades, technological development has increased the demand for skilled workers to the detriment of less-skilled workers, pushing up the income of more-educated workers and lowering the income of less-educated workers [2, 47]. Advances in telecommunication and transport technologies give a small number of qualified workers the opportunity to expand their local markets and receive higher wages and benefits [49]. Therefore, technology not only lowers the income of uneducated workers but also creates more opportunities for the educated workforce. In addition, globalization has interconnected the world economies and has put the less-educated workers in developed countries in direct competition with their counterparts in low-wage developing countries [2]. Another important factor that could explain the increasing inequality is sectoral shifts. According to this view, the shifts from agriculture to industry and then from industry to service in the past three decades have led to an increase in economic inequality [49]. One explanation is that the service sector usually has a lower union density than industry and manufacturing [49].

The cyclical nature of capitalistic economies and the recurring financial crisis often hit the low and middle classes hardest and bring them the highest levels of indebtedness [50]. On the contrary, the rich not only are immune to periodic financial crises but also can take advantage of economic downturns to acquire assets such as real estate and equities at discount prices. The super-rich have the sufficient capital to spend on the best investment, on the tax or legal advice, and on the estate planning. The wealth held by the super-rich since the financial crisis of 2007 to 2008 has been growing annually by an average of 11 percent [32]. Despite their donations, the super-rich exert a destructive impact on the society simply by pursuing the higher levels of capital accumulation. Debt and fortune both grow exponentially; once a fortune or debt is accumulated it gains momentum and grows automatically. That is why the gap between the rich and the poor tends to grow over time unless some effective policies are put in place.

The economic inequality, particularly in the United States, is an outcome of government policies regarding minimum wage, income tax code, health care, education, and social programs. According to the Urban Institute-Brookings Institution Tax Policy Center, tax cuts that benefit the most affluent are one of the main culprits of the deepening economic disparities [3]. For instance, during the 1980s due to Ronald Reagan's policies, income taxes became less progressive. A few years later under George W. Bush presidency, some major tax cuts allowed the households with incomes more than $200,000 to receive bigger write-offs for their mortgage interests. The International Monetary Fund reports show that tax systems in the United States and around the world have become gradually less progressive since the early 1980s, via the lowering of the top rate of income tax, cuts to taxes on capital gains, and reductions in inheritance and wealth taxes [23]. Indeed, many countries are continuing to reduce their taxes on the rich in order to attract more investment. The rich can buy the right to permanent residency in many countries such as the United Kingdom, the United States, Canada, Australia, and Malta with $500,000 to $2 million. In addition to tax cuts, the U.S. governments under Ronald Reagan and George W. Bush have taken measures to reduce the funding for social programs that benefit the poor such as Medicaid, food stamps, affordable health care, and more importantly education [3]. Education yields higher returns in advanced societies and thus plays an important role in creating a more egalitarian society. Nevertheless, the access to higher education has become even more difficult and more expensive in the recent years.

In general, the government policies have focused on fighting inflation and unemployment and finance has played a central role in the American economy. As a result, manufacturing jobs have declined, labor unions have weakened, and the link between workers' productivity and compensation has become less relevant. Workers' unions aim at maintaining consistent wage differentials between skilled and unskilled workers. Therefore, the rapid declines of unionization in the UK and the United States since the 1980s have contributed to the rising levels of economic inequality [48]. While many high-ranking managers have seen colossal rises in their revenues, wages for frontline workers have hardly increased. The big businesses continue to benefit the rich and deprive the poor of the positives outcomes of economic growth and wealth creation [22]. The frontline workers who are responsible for much of the productivity are not compensated proportionately to their contributions. By contrast, many chief executives receive generous compensation packages equivalent to the wages of thousands of their hardworking employees [32].

In an era of business globalization, low-wage workers across the world see their wages pressed by global supply chains where suppliers compete to provide consumers with the lowest prices. Using the new information technology, the corporations are able to closely monitor their workers, increase pressure on them, and squeeze down the cost of production. All workers particularly blue-collars are facing harsher working conditions and less bargaining power as the proportion of the unionized workforce has fallen by nearly 50 percent in the past four decades [12]. Such savings are passed to the top executives and shareholders, while the ordinary workers do not benefit at all. In other words, the big corporations are enriching the rich to the detriment of the poor and thus are contributing to the economic inequality [25]. Furthermore, corporations use their connections to secure lax regulations and lower tax rates that benefit the rich at the expense of the rest. While ordinary people pay more than their fair share, the crony capitalists are accumulating wealth and power.

Though the rich are actively spending a lot of money to influence the political process, the poor often do not participate in elections to exert their most basic right as citizens. The rise of economic inequality has disappointed the poor and underprivileged voters [14]. For example, 9 out of 10 individuals in families with incomes over $75,000 vote in presidential elections while only half of those in families with incomes under $15,000 reported voting [14]. Therefore, American elections are becoming the privileges of the rich to elect those who protect their interests.

The economic inequality could be linked to culture, as some societies attach importance to egalitarianism whereas others accept and even promote disparity. For example, there are significant cultural differences between the Europeans and Americans with regard to economic inequality. The Europeans tend to be more egalitarian and see the high levels of economic disparity with suspicion. By contrast, Americans fully support private ownership and tend to see economic disparities as the natural consequences of differences in individual talent and effort. These cultural differences may explain why the United States is ranked as the most economically unequal nation among the Western industrialized countries.

The Consequences of Inequality

On the one hand, the rising levels of economic inequality could create incentives for the majority of people to work harder to materialize their financial objectives and ultimately get richer. According to this premise, economic inequality leads to efficiency, creativity, and entrepreneurship. On the other hand, the higher levels of inequality imply that the rich are better positioned to take advantage of economic opportunities than the rest of the population do. As the rich actively aim at increasing their wealth, they use their power to create exclusive entitlements and privileges for themselves and deprive the rest of the society of similar opportunities in the job market, education, and investment. Extreme inequality necessarily reduces the social mobility, so if you are born poor you will end your life in poverty (Figure 9.7). As Krugman (2007, p. 249) noticed: "A society with highly unequal results is, more or less inevitably, a society with highly unequal opportunity, too" [51]. Therefore, we may suggest that, while a certain level of inequality motivates economic growth by rewarding hard work and innovation, the extreme levels of inequality could curb the economic growth and cause inefficiencies [33].

Children's likelihood of earning more than their parents
by birth year and income percentile

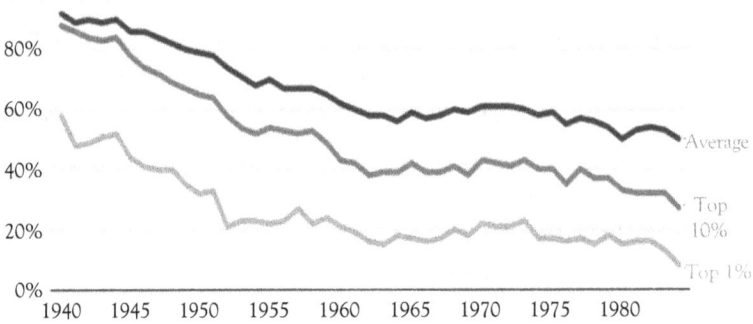

Chart by mother jones

Figure 9.7 Attaining the "American Dream" has become more difficult over time

The concentration of wealth in the hands of a small number of people depresses spending, demand, and economic growth [34]. When wealth is more evenly distributed across the population, it would provide a large number of people with spending power, which in turn would boost economic growth and wealth creation [43]. There are some indications that the extreme levels of inequality could lead to financial crises [53, 54]. The recent academic research has shown four major paths by which inequality can cause the economic instability and financial crisis: (1) weak demand, (2) rising household debt and asset bubbles, (3) debt-led growth and international imbalances, and (4) financial speculation [53]. Income inequality often causes a sluggishness of demand since lower income groups do not have the sufficient resources to spend and consume. Extreme inequality implies that a large number of people rely progressively on debt to pay for their essential needs. As the levels of individual or household debt increase, the financial system becomes unstable. In other words, poverty or insufficient income creates unpayable debt that ultimately shakes the financial system. Furthermore, the debt-led growth in countries such as the United States and the United Kingdom fueled economy artificially and created asset bubbles that were essentially unsustainable. Furthermore, the concentrated wealth at the top generally is more likely to be spent in speculation activities that in turn could involve financial instability.

Wealth is power and, like any form of power, it causes corruption. The bigger the wealth, the bigger is the level of corruption. The rise of economic inequality creates opportunities for the super-rich to abuse of their wealth directly or indirectly. The extreme levels of economic inequality pose a substantial threat to democracy and the rule of law. Even in the democracies such as the United States, the rich spend large amounts of money on shifting the elections outcomes, lobbying politicians, and affecting the political process [42]. Joseph Stiglitz, a prominent American economist and a professor at Columbia University, examined the relationship between the financial industry and the centers of political power in countries such as the United States and the United Kingdom [35]. His analyses reveal that the conservative parties are highly affected by the donations from the financial industry [36]. In the U.S. elections, billionaires provide funding to influence the political decision making and support their favored candidates. Other wealthy individuals openly support some political causes and intervene in the political process. For example, the Koch brothers, two American billionaires, have exerted a significant influence over the Republican Party in the United States and have supported Tea Party movement [32]. Some wealthy individuals directly have run for office in countries such as Georgia, India, Italy, Lebanon, the Philippines, Russia, Ukraine, and the United States [52]. Simply put, the rich can buy votes. The elections represent the dollar values, not the voters' numbers. The impact of the rich on the political process is much more widespread in developing countries due to their weak institutions and rampant corruption. So, it is obvious that inequality has some grave consequences for democracy and the rule of law. A strong middle class is a prerequisite for a stable democracy because, when the majority has insufficient resources to support its demands, the cost of oppression is reduced for the rich [9, 54]. In other words, a more equitable distribution of wealth and property empowers the majority of the population to defend their legitimate rights through democratically established institutions.

The rich afford a better education, an excellence health care, and superior professional services. Thus, they are more likely to occupy higher offices and enrich themselves even more, while the poor flounder to make a living as they go deeper and deeper in financial obligations. The super-rich evade taxes by putting their wealth in tax havens or tax-sheltered accounts. They might also rely on secretive services or legal loopholes to dodge taxes and deprive the government/nation of their fair share. It is estimated that $7.6 trillion of wealth is hidden offshore in tax heavens [31].

Extreme inequality dents social cohesiveness and reduces the social mobility. In the past three decades, the social mobility has sharply fallen in the United States, so one could attain the American dream much easier in Sweden than in the United States [52]. Extreme inequality causes various sociocultural problems such as crime, gun violence, mental disorder, and obesity [38]. Simply put, economic disparities leave more people living in fear and fewer in hope [25]. Empirical studies have shown that inequality has some negative implications for the health and well-being of people at all levels of income and wealth brackets [39]. For example, it is reported that the risks of infectious diseases and heart-related problems are higher in the countries marked by extreme levels of economic inequality. By contrast, the health status of people in the more egalitarian countries tends to be better at all income levels [9, 55]. In addition, extreme inequality has significant damaging effects on the environment. Some studies have shown that the egalitarian countries are more likely to reduce carbon emissions and protect the physical environment [40]. According to a recent report by the World Bank, countries with more equal distribution of wealth enjoy a more sustainable growth [41].

The Plutocrats or the Global Super-Rich

Beyond the top 1 percent of the richest people who are mostly multimillionaires, there is a new group of super-rich billionaires or "plutocrats" who are representing only 0.1 percent of the population. According to the 2016 Forbes list, 1,810 billionaires own between $6.5 and $7 trillion or as much wealth as the bottom 70 percent of humanity [21]. Wealth continues to accumulate for the super-rich as their returns on investment often surpass economic growth. The distance between the super-rich and the rich (multimillionaires) has been widening fast for the past three decades. Ironically, the deepening divide is no longer between the rich and the poor; rather it is between the rich and the super-rich [57]. The gap between the rich and the poor is obviously very huge, but the one between the super-rich and the rest of the population is even much bigger. For instance, while the average earnings of the top 1 percent are 15 times the income received by 90 percent of the population, the average earnings of the super-rich is 124 times higher [57]. This is a major socio-economic shift because the super-rich can put pressure not only on the middle-class citizens but also on the multimillionaires, on the rich!

It is estimated that half of the super-rich individuals are from the United States and the rest of the Western Europe or countries such as China, Brazil, Mexico, Japan, and Saudi Arabia [56]. The super-rich often originates in two parts of the world namely Western countries and emerging markets. According to Forbes magazine, there are almost 492 billionaires in America with a combined net worth of more than $2 trillion. The number of billionaires in Europe is estimated at 468 including 85 in Germany, 47 in the United Kingdom, 43 in France, 35 in Italy, and 26 in Spain with a combined wealth of $1.95 trillion [52]. Most of the super-rich have benefited from a combination of the technological revolution and globalization. The super-rich may consist of the technology elite in Silicon Valley, Wall Street financial sharks, Russian oligarchs, and investment geniuses [57]. The CEOs and CFOs are at the top of the list. Indeed, 40 percent of Americans making over $30 million per year come from the corporate and financial sectors. The recent revolution in telecommunication technology has been a key driver in the rise of the global super-rich who are often self-made, highly educated, and mainly young. The super-rich have the privileges and the abilities to effectively take advantage of the emerging social and economic trends and maximize their fortunes. Mark Zuckerberg, Steve Jobs, Jim Rogers, George Soros, Jeff Bezos, and Bill Gates are the prime examples of those who detected the opportunities and responded quickly. For these entrepreneurs, the crises are translated to the best business opportunities. More importantly, the super-rich take advantage of economic and political systems thanks to their proximity to the centers of decision making. In general, the rent-seeking activities do not contribute any values to the economy but serve as shortcuts to wealth accumulation. India, Russia, Brazil, Mexico, South Africa, China, and many other emerging markets are the favorite places of the super-rich rent-seekers. For example, Carlos Slim, one of the richest men in the world with a wealth of more than $50 billion, built his fortune by using his telecommunication companies to influence and exploit the Mexican privatization process [57]. In the United States, the rent-seekers include bankers, hedge-fund managers, CEOs, CFOs, and all those who use their privileged positions to exploit the stock-market imperfections or to commit insider trading.

The super-rich have generally benefited from strong business connections, have studied at prestigious schools, and have accumulated their wealth in their youth. Most of them lead major charitable organizations designed to take advantages of new opportunities, to dodge taxes, enhance their reputations, and above all to twist the rules and regulations. The super-rich aim at influencing the world and all aspects of social and even personal life comprising economics, politics, education, culture, art, and nutrition. Emboldened by their vast personal wealth, the super-rich are convinced that their opinions are necessarily beneficial to the society, are engaged in social activities, and seek to promulgate their own worldview. They purchase major news outlets and provide considerable funding for political organizations [52]. The Bill & Melinda Gates Foundation, the Chan Zuckerberg Initiative, and the Soros Open Society Foundations are examples of the super-rich organizations that are intervening in all spheres of our personal and social life. In 2015, Mark Zuckerberg and his wife Priscilla Chan vowed to donate 99 percent of their Facebook shares to "the cause of human advancement" [58]. Pursuing the cause of human advancement is a euphemism for accumulating more power and wealth. The political and social activism of the super-rich does not receive enough coverage and remains mainly secretive. As the super-rich get more powerful and aim at influencing different aspects of political and economic systems, they represent a significant threat to the democratic rule and the stability of our societies as a whole [57]. The super-rich, whether they are value-creators or rent-seekers, is becoming too powerful to be subject to an effective supervisory structure and legal framework. Simply put, the super-rich are changing the rules instead of abiding by them.

The Popular Myths About Wealth and Poverty

There are certain popular myths about wealth, poverty, and inequality that should be debunked as they continue to mislead the ordinary citizens.

The first myth is about the function of the market. In undergraduate textbooks, students often learn about the rule of supply and demand and make the false assumption that there is a wise and invisible hand behind every market; therefore, the market is always right and self-sufficient. Based on this wrong assumption, some suggest that the role and involvement of government in business should be eliminated or at least minimized. Indeed, no market operates in a vacuum. Every market consists of different participants that affect the prices by their interests. During the past decade, we have witnessed how greed, fear, corruption, cronyism, and abuse of power have led to financial crises and led to government intervention [25]. If unregulated, businesses in the areas such as telecommunication and the Internet, finance and banking, health care, aviation, education, infrastructure, and public safety could severely stifle the small competitors and harm the underprivileged customers. The collapse of the American banking system in 2007 and 2008 pushed the Federal Reserve to hand out colossal amounts of money to the ailing banks and bail them out by the taxpayers' money [59]. If the markets were self-sufficient, then why did the government intervene in the market and bail them out? Some may answer that the American banks were too big to fail and their failure could have triggered a worldwide depression [60]. This argument refutes the principle of market self-sufficiency because it implies that governments should intervene in the market and regulate the banks by preventing them from becoming too big. At any rate, in banking, we need the intervention of government, either by regulating the banks and preventing them from becoming too big or by bailing them out when they are too big to fail.

Another prevalent myth about wealth and poverty is the idea that extreme economic inequality is justified because individual wealth is a sign of success and hard work. Despite abundant evidence, this wrong assumption is strongly supported by most of Americans [24]. Obviously, some degrees of economic disparity are normal as they correlate with individual success and effort, but extreme levels of economic inequality are the results of a dysfunctional economy where individual effort does not lead to success and prosperity. The super-rich gains too much power that can undermine the institutions, the rule of law, and democratic systems. Because of the extreme degrees of economic inequality, a large number of citizens are deprived of their basic needs like a decent level of education, health care, training, housing, and nutrition. Furthermore, the extreme degrees of economic inequality reduce social mobility and affect the economic productivity negatively. The super-rich often abuses their vast resources to increase their wealth and influence. They continue to enrich themselves without any effort or value creation.

Another popular myth is the notion that businesses exist to maximize their profits at all costs. While the profit maximization is the raison d'etre of any business, it is important to pay attention to all stakeholders including customers, communities, suppliers, and workers. No business is sustainable unless it has access to reliable workforce, institutions, communities, and customers. When businesses are involved in rent-seeking activities, they may excessively boost the shareholders' gains to the detriment of all other stakeholders. Therefore, the economic inequality rises as the shareholders and managers get richer whereas the ordinary workers and customers continue to get poorer.

A false assumption about the concentration of wealth and economic inequality is the notion that business and trade are not zero-sum games and everybody can become rich. According to this perspective, we should not criticize the economic inequality; rather, we should avoid envy and instead focus on hard work. The fact of the matter is that everything including wealth is relative and business is essentially a zero-sum game that has some losers and some winners. The accumulation of wealth on the one side necessarily causes poverty on the other side.

Another prevalent assumption is the idea that minorities and women can become as wealthy as others do. In other words, economic inequality is not about race, ethnicity, and gender. As mentioned earlier, the minorities, women, and children are the main victims of economic inequality. In 2007, the median wealth for single women between the ages of 18 and 64 was $15,210 or 49 percent of the median wealth of their single male counterparts. Single women of color and women with children are in a worse financial situation. Despite significant progress in the recent years, there are enormous obstacles to the full participation of minorities and women. In many countries, women continue to receive lower salaries than their male counterparts do. Therefore, the extreme economic inequality is not a matter of effort or talent only; it is deeply rooted in race, ethnicity, gender, and birthplace.

References

[1] Kalleberg, A.L. 2009. "Precarious Work, Insecure Workers: Employment Relations in Transition." *American Sociological Review* 74, no. 1, pp. 1–22.

[2] Schmitt, J. 2009. *Inequality as Policy: The United States since 1979*. Center for Economic Policy Research, October.

[3] Tritch, T. 2006. *The Rise of the Super-rich*, 19. New York Times.

[4] Kawachi, I., and B.P. Kennedy. 2002. *The Health of Nations: Why Inequality is Harmful to Your Health*. New York: The New Press.

[5] Piketty, T., and E. Saez. 2003. "Income Inequality in the United States, 1913–1998." *Quarterly Journal of Economics* CXVII, pp. 1–39.

[6] Reich, R.B. 2007. *Supercapitalism*. New York: Barzoi Books.

[7] Hacker, J.S. 2007. "The New Economic Insecurity—and What Can be Done about it." *Harvard Law and Policy Review* 1, pp. 111–26.

[8] Warren, E., and A.W. Tyagi. 2003. *The Two-Income Trap: Why Middle-Class Parents are Going Broke*. New York: Basic Books.

[9] Littrell, J., F. Brooks, J. Ivery, and M.L. Ohmer. 2010. "Why You Should Care about the Threatened Middle Class." *J. Soc. & Soc. Welfare* 37, p. 87.

[10] O'Loughlin, J. 1997. "Economic Globalization and Income Inequality in the United States." *State Devolution in America: Implications for a Diverse Society*, pp. 21–40.

[11] DeSilver, D. 2013. "Global Inequality: How the U.S. Compares." Pew Research Center, Retrieved December 19, 2013 from http://pewresearch. org/fact-tank/2013/12/19/global-inequality-how-the-u-s-compares/

[12] Statistical Abstract on the web site of the U.S. Bureau of the Census (www. census.gov/statab/).

[13] Smeeding, T.M. "Public Policy and Economic Inequality: The United States in Comparative Perspective." Paper prepared for Campbell Institute Seminar, "Inequality and American Democracy," February 20, 2004. www.maxwell.syr.edu/campbell/Events/Smeeding.pdf

[14] Freeman, R.B. 2003. What, Me Vote? (No. w9896). National Bureau of Economic Research.

[15] Skocpol, T. 2004. *American Democracy in an Age of Rising Inequality*. The American Political Science Association

[16] Haughton, J., and S.R. Khandker. 2009. *Handbook on Poverty + Inequality*. World Bank Publications.

[17] Morin, R. 2012. *Rising Share of Americans See a Conflict Between Rich and Poor*, 11. Pew Research Center.

[18] Gabler, N. 2016. "The Secret Shame of Middle-Class Americans." *The Atlantic*, pp. 53–63.

[19] DeSa, U.N. 2013. "Inequality Matters." Report on the World Social Situation 2013. New York, United Nations.

[20] Nguyen T.L. 2017. *Even It Up: How to Tackle Inequality in Vietnam.* Oxford: Oxfam. http://oxf.am/ZLuU

[21] Forbes 2016. "The World's Billionaires." http://forbes.com/billionaires/list/

[22] Rhodes, F., J. Burnley, M. Dolores, J. Kyriacou, R. Wilshaw, D. Ukhova, and M. Talpur. 2016. *Underpaid and Undervalued: How Inequality Defines Women's Work in Asia.* Oxford: Oxfam. http://policy-practice.oxfam.org.uk/publications/underpaid-and-undervalued-how-inequality-defines-womens-work-in-asia-611297

[23] IMF 2014. "The IMF Finds that Reductions in the Generosity of Benefits and Less Progressive Taxation have Decreased the Redistributive Impact of Fiscal Policy Since the mid-1990s." Fiscal Policy and Income Inequality. https://imf.org/external/np/pp/eng/2014/012314.pdf

[24] Jacobs, D. 2015. "Extreme Wealth Is Not Merited." Op. cit; The Economist. Crony-Capitalism Index. http://economist.com/news/international/21599041-countries-where-politically-connected-businessmen-are-most-likely-prosper-planet

[25] Hardoon, D. 2017. An Economy for the 99%: It's Time to Build a Human Economy that Benefits Everyone, Not Just the Privileged Few.

[26] Credit Suisse. 2016. "Global Wealth Databook." http://publications.credit-suisse.com/tasks/render/file/index.cfm?fileid=AD6F2B43-B17B-345E-E20A1A254A3E24A5

[27] Hardoon, D., S. Ayele, and R. Fuentes-Nieva. 2016. *An Economy for the 1%.* Oxford: Oxfam. http://policy-practice.oxfam.org.uk/publications/an-economy-for-the-1-how-privilege-and-power-in-the-economy-drive-extreme-inequ-592643

[28] Oxfam Calculations Using the Wealth of the Richest Individuals from Forbes Billionaires Listing and Wealth of the Bottom 50% from Credit Suisse Global Wealth Databook 2016.

[29] Calculations by Ergon Associates Using CEO Pay Data from the High Pay Centre and the Minimum Wage of a Bangladeshi Worker Plus Typical Benefits Packages Offered to Workers.

[30] Rhodes, F., J. Burnley, M. Dolores, J. Kyriacou, R. Wilshaw, D. Ukhova, L. Gibson, and M. Talpur 2016. *Underpaid and Undervalued: How Inequality Defines Women's Work in Asia.* Oxford: Oxfam. http://policy-practice.oxfam.org.uk/publications/underpaid-and-undervalued-how-inequality-defines-womens-work-in-asia-611297

[31] Zuchman, G. 2015. *The Hidden Wealth of Nations.* University of Chicago Press. https://doi.org/10.7208/chicago/9780226645560.001.0001

[32] Mayer, J. 2016. "Dark Money: The Hidden History of the Billionaires Behind the Rise of the Radical Right." https://amazon.com/Dark-Money-History-Billionaires-Radical/dp/0385535597/ref=la_B000APC6Q6_1_1/154-3729860-5160132?s=books&ie=UTF8&qid=1480689221&sr=1-1

[33] Berg, A.G., and J.D. Osrty. 2013. "Inequality and Unsustainable Growth: Two Sides of the Same Coin?." *International Organisations Research Journal* 8, no. 4, pp. 77–99.

[34] Ford Company Report. http://corporate.ford.com/news-center/press-releases-detail/677-5-dollar-a-day

[35] Hacker, J.S., and P. Pierson. 2010. *Winner-Take-All Politics: How Washington Made the Rich Richer--and Turned its Back on the Middle Class.* Simon and Schuster.

[36] Syal, R., J. Treanor, and N. Mathiason. 2011. "City's Influence Over Conservatives Laid Bare by Research into Donations." *The Guardian.*

[37] Smiley, T. 2012. *The Rich and the Rest of Us.* Hay House, Inc.

[38] Wilkinson, R.G., and K.E. Pickett. 2009. "Income Inequality and Social Dysfunction." *Annual Review of Sociology* 35, pp. 493–511.

[39] Wilkinson, R.G., and K. Pickett. 2009. *The Spirit Level: Why an Equal Societies Almost Always Do Better,* 6 vols. London: Allen Lane.

[40] Grunewald, N., S. Klasen, I. Martínez-Zarzoso, and C. Muris. 2012. Income Inequality and Carbon Emissions.

[41] World Bank. 2005. *World Development Report 2006: Equity and Development.* Oxford University Press, Incorporated.

[42] Slater, J. 2013. *The Cost of Inequality: How Wealth and Income Extremes Hurt us All.* Oxfam.

[43] Lowrey, A. 2012. "Income Inequality May Take a Toll on Growth." *New York Times* 16, no. 10.

[44] Cornia, G.A., and T. Addison. 2003. "Income Distribution Changes and Their Impact in the Post-World War II Period." World Institute for Development Economics Research Discussion Paper No. 2003/28.

[45] Lakner, C. 2016. Global Inequality: The Implications of Thomas Piketty's Capital in the 21st Century.

[46] Ortiz, I., and M. Cummins. 2011. Global Inequality: Beyond the Bottom Billion–A Rapid Review of Income Distribution in 141 Countries.

[47] Alderson, A.S., and K. Doran. 2010. "How has Income Inequality Grown? The Reshaping of the Income Distribution in LIS Countries." Inequality and the Status of the Middle Class: Lessons from the Luxembourg Income Study, Luxembourg.

[48] Acemoglu, D., P. Aghion, and G.L. Violante. December 2001. "Deunionization, Technical Change, and Inequality." In *Carnegie-Rochester Conference Series on Public Policy* 55, no. 1, pp. 229–64. North-Holland.

[49] Allison, C., E. Fleisje, W. Glevey, and W.L. Johannes. 2014. *Trends and Key Drivers of Income Inequality*. Marshall Economic Research Group, University of Cambridge.

[50] Streeck, W. 2014. "The Politics of Public Debt: Neoliberalism, Capitalist Development and the Restructuring of the State." *German Economic Review* 15, no. 1, pp. 143–65.

[51] OECD. Publishing. 2015. *In It Together: Why Less Inequality Benefits All.* OECD Publishing.

[52] West, D.M. 2014. "Wealthification in the United States and Europe." *Intereconomics* 49, no. 5, pp. 295–96.

[53] Martin, A., T. Greenham, and H. Kersley. 2014. *Inequality and Financialization: A Dangerous Mix*. New Economics Foundation.

[54] Acemoglu, D., and J.A. Robinson. 2005. *Economic Origins of Dictatorship and Democracy*. Cambridge University Press.

[55] Babones, S.J. 2008. "Income Inequality and Population Health: Correlation and Causality." *Social Science & Medicine* 66, no. 7, pp. 1614–26.

[56] Fuentes-Nieva, R., and N. Galasso. 2014. *Working for the Few: Political Capture and Economic Inequality*, 178 vols. Oxfam.

[57] Freeland, C. 2012. *Plutocrats: The Rise of the New Global Super-rich and the Fall of Everyone Else*. Penguin.

[58] Mark Zuckerberg is Giving Away His Money, but With a Twist. http://fortune.com/2015/12/02/zuckerberg-charity/

[59] https://economist.com/news/schoolsbrief/21584534-effects-financial-crisis-are-still-being-felt-five-years-article

[60] Ingram, M. 2015. "Mark Zuckerberg Is Giving Away His Money, But With a Twist." *Fortune,* December.

CHAPTER 10

The Global Health and Well-Being

1. The Increasing Life Expectancy and Aging Populations
2. The Increased Incidence of Noncommunicable Diseases
3. The Risks of Pandemics
4. The Rising Cost of Care and Shortage of Health Care Workers
5. The Transformation of Social Insurance Systems

Increasing Life Expectancy and Aging Populations

Astonishing increases in life expectancy in tandem with falling fertility rates are changing the world demographic landscape drastically. In the past 50 years, life expectancy at birth has been growing steadily across the world from an average of 46.5 years in 1955 to 65.2 years in 2002. This degree of improvement in life expectancy varies from 9 years in developed countries to 17 years in the high-mortality developing countries including most of Africa and Asia to 26 years in the low-mortality developing countries [1] (Figure 10.1). The improvement in human life expectancy started more than 150 years ago in Europe because of multiple factors including improvement in nutrition, housing, sanitation, hygiene, education, and the new advances in science and technology. Until the mid-19th century, the risk of death was high at a young age and, consequently, only a small proportion of people could reach old age. By contrast, in our modern societies, deaths often happen at older ages. In the recent decades, the health status of adults across the world has improved substantially and, as a result, the risk of death between ages 15 and 60 has dropped from 354 per 1,000 in 1955 to 207 per 1,000 in 2002 [1]. Despite all these achievements, there are significant gaps between life expectancy at birth in the developed nations and the least developed

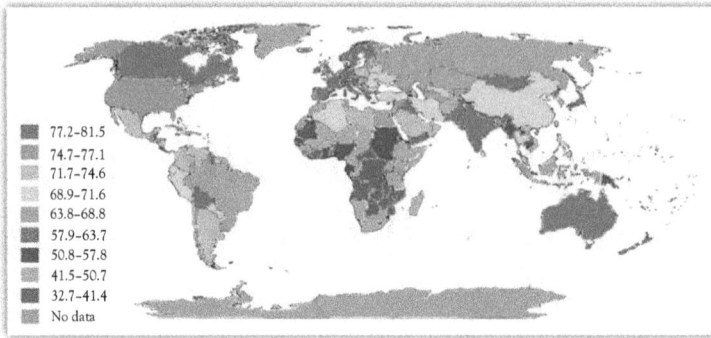

Figure 10.1 *Average life expectancy across the globe (years)*

Source: Adapted from Global Education Project. 2004. Human Conditions: World Life Expectancy Map. Retrieved from http://theglobaleducationproject.org/earth/human-conditions.php

countries of Sub-Saharan Africa. For instance, in early 2000, life expectancy at birth could vary from 78 years for women in developed countries to less than 46 years for men in Sub-Saharan Africa [1]. In developed countries almost 80 percent of adult deaths happen after 60 years of age; however, this ratio is 42 percent in the case of developing countries [1].

An interesting trend is that while the developed countries will have the oldest population structure, the fastest aging populations and the massive majority of older people will reside in less developed countries in the next four decades (Figure 10.2). Between 2010 and 2050, the number of older people in developing countries could increase more than 250 percent, compared with a 71 percent increase in developed countries [2]. In 2010, an estimated 524 million people were aged 65 or older representing 8 percent of the world's population. By 2050, the number of people aged 65 or older will triple to reach 1.5 billion or almost 16 percent of the world's population [9]. Since most of the longevity improvement is happening in the developing countries of Asia and Africa, most of the growth in the aging population is expected to be seen in such countries. In East Asia, life expectancy at birth improved from less than 45 years in 1950 to more than 74 years now. Consequently, China and India as the world's two most populous countries will experience the highest increases in the number of senior people. In China alone, the number of people aged 65 and more will surge from 110 million in 2015 to 330 million in 2050. Likewise, India's senior population will grow from 60 million in 2015 to more than 227 million in 2050 [2]. In addition to sharp increases in the

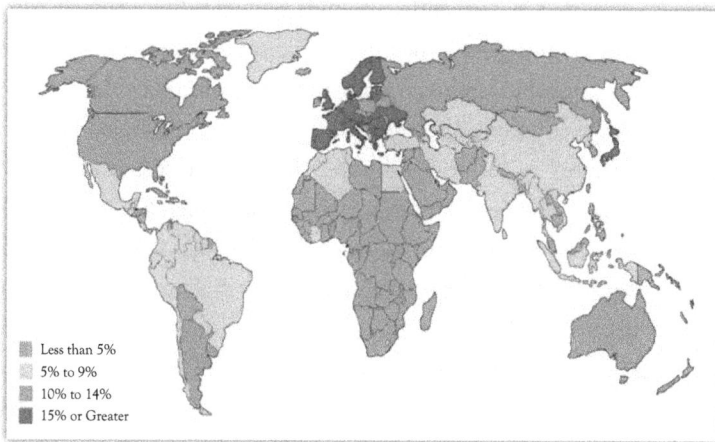

Figure 10.2 Percentage of population aged 65 or older, 2007

Source: Adapted from Population Reference Bureau. 2007. 2007 World Population Data Sheet.
Retrieved from http://prb.org/pdf07/07WPDS_Eng.pdf

number of people over 65 years old, there will be a global surge in the number of the "oldest-old" or those aged over 80 [15]. The number of the oldest-old is expected to rise from 90 million today to more than 400 million in 2050, representing 4 percent of the global population by 2050 [7]. By 2050, China could have more than 100 million people over the age of 80. The rapid aging of the U.S. population is so amazing that, by 2050, the number of Americans aged 65 and more will reach 90 million or more than twice the number in 2010 [3].

The increasing levels of life expectancy and the swelling aging populations require that both developed and developing countries take adequate measures to maintain or improve the effectiveness of their health and social care systems [15]. The health-related consequences of these changes are various and may include increased rates of noncommunicable illnesses such as cancer, dementia, diabetes, cardiovascular diseases, a potential shortage of health care workers/resources, and increasing numbers of people needing long-term care.

The Increased Incidence of Noncommunicable Diseases

As the world's societies undergo economic development, they see significant declines in the rates of mortality and fertility, and improvements in life expectancy. Consequently, an epidemiologic shift happens in the pattern of disease and death. The infectious diseases lose their importance as the main causes of mortality whereas the noncommunicable or chronic diseases become common. In the early 20th century, the major sources of death were related to infectious diseases that often targeted infants and children. Today, noncommunicable diseases that touch adults and older people represent a major threat to the public health. Nevertheless, high mortality rates from infectious diseases are still prevalent in less developed countries because of the abject poverty, lack of sanitation, and malnutrition. As these countries undergo socioeconomic development, they are expected to see lower rates of mortality associated with infectious and parasitic diseases. Therefore, a considerable trend in the contemporary world is the increased incidence of noncommunicable diseases in both developed and developing countries [2]. The main categories of noncommunicable diseases are related to older age groups and include cardiovascular diseases, cancers, chronic respiratory diseases and asthma, diabetes, and mental disorders. It is estimated that over the next 10 to 15 years, people in every world region will suffer more death and disability from such noncommunicable diseases than from infectious and parasitic diseases.

According to the World Health Organization, a variety of factors such as rapid and unplanned urbanization, globalization of unhealthy lifestyles, population aging, unhealthy diets, tobacco and alcohol addiction, and a lack of physical activity can cause the noncommunicable diseases. Furthermore, environmental degradation, exposure to air and water pollution, genetically modified organisms and new food processing techniques, dependence on smartphones, overconsumption of sugar, fat, and salt, and many other manifestations of our modern hectic lifestyles increase the risks of noncommunicable diseases [4]. Obesity is an important risk factor for many noncommunicable diseases and conditions, including stroke, heart disease, cancer, and arthritis [5]. According to the National Health and Nutrition Examination Survey, the prevalence of obesity among older adults is estimated at 34.6 percent in the United States [6].

In 2008, noncommunicable diseases accounted for 86 percent of diseases in high-income countries, 65 percent in middle-income countries, and 37 percent in low-income countries. By 2030, the shares of noncommunicable diseases in middle- and low-income countries will increase respectively to 75 and 50 percent. By contrast, infectious and parasitic diseases will account for 10 and 30 percent in middle- and low-income countries, respectively [2]. According to the World Health Organization, noncommunicable diseases are responsible for the death of 40 million people each year representing 70 percent of all deaths. Cardiovascular diseases with 17.7 million deaths per year account for most deaths caused by noncommunicable diseases, followed by cancers (8.8 million), respiratory diseases (3.9 million), and diabetes (1.6 million).

Noncommunicable diseases imply some serious social and economic consequences. At the individual level, noncommunicable diseases lead the patients and their families to poverty, pain, and bankruptcy. It is estimated that about 100 million patients in the world fall into poverty every year due to the costs associated with their treatment [6]. Many businesses and organizations are affected adversely as their workforce lose productivity or are eliminated. The World Economic Forum (2008) estimated that the emerging economies such as Brazil, China, India, South Africa, and Russia might have lost more than 20 million productive life years due to cardiovascular diseases in 2000. Obviously, the impact of all types of noncommunicable diseases in future will be much more significant as the number of the patients continue to grow drastically. The economic losses of noncommunicable diseases could reach $47 trillion in the next two decades hindering the economic growth and prosperity across the world.

Mental disorders such as dementia and Alzheimer's are other prevalent noncommunicable diseases that are affecting the lives of a large number of people and are often associated with old age. Dementia could have various causes and symptoms, but this disease is often associated with a loss of memory, reasoning, and other cognitive capacities [2]. Dementia, especially in its early stages, is difficult to diagnose and very frequently it remains undiagnosed and underreported even in developed countries. For that reason, the data about the prevalence of dementia across the world are not standard and reliable. Based on the Organization for Economic Cooperation and Development (OECD) reports in 2000, dementia affected about 10 million people in OECD member countries representing 7 percent of people aged 65 or older. Alzheimer's disease is the most common form of dementia and accounted for between two-fifths and four-fifths of all dementia cases. Currently, the number of people affected by dementia is estimated between 27 and 36 million across the world [2]. The prevalence of dementia is very low at a younger age but it increases sharply after age 65. Based on the OECD studies, only 3 percent of people between ages 65 and 69 were affected by dementia, while the proportion for those between 85 and 89 reached 30 percent. Similar studies in France and Germany showed that more than half of women aged 90 or older had some forms of dementia [2]. The studies by the Alzheimer's Disease International suggest that by 2050 there will be around 115 million people worldwide living with Alzheimer's or dementia [2]. As the world's population is getting older, the number of affected people is expected to put mounting pressure on health care providers, families, and governments across the world. According to the World Alzheimer Report, the total worldwide cost of dementia was estimated more than US$600 billion in 2010 [2]. The cost associated with dementia is expected to rise exponentially, especially in low- and middle-income countries that have insufficient resources for mental health allocating less than 2 percent of their health budget to the treatment and prevention of this disease [4]. Most of the people affected by dementia eventually lose their independence and need constant help with their daily activities causing a heavy economic and social burden on their families and communities [2]. As families become smaller and people have fewer children, there will be fewer family members to look after elderly people affected by dementia.

The Risks of Pandemics

Throughout the history, the world has experienced devastating epidemics of communicable diseases such as smallpox, cholera, typhoid, and measles causing the death of millions of people. For example, an outbreak of influenza killed around 50 million people in 1918. Despite all the advances in medicine and public health, many communicable diseases still claim millions of lives. Malaria, tuberculosis, HIV/AIDS, bacterial diarrhea, and cholera are among the deadliest communicable diseases affecting a large number of people and causing a million deaths annually across the world, particularly in low- and middle-income countries.

Poverty may be considered one of the main causes of communicable disease outbreaks. In many developing countries, sanitary and hygiene standards are extremely low, and a large number of people do not have access to clean water. According to a report by the World Health Organization and Unicef, a third of the world's population do not have access to adequate toilets [16]. Half the population of India or around 564 million people do not have proper sanitation and defecate in the open, excreting close to 65,000 tons of feces into the environment each day. The open defecation practice is responsible for 188,000 deaths of children under five in India each year [17]. The malnutrition due to poverty is believed to contribute to the spread of communicable diseases through deteriorating the immune system. Furthermore, low levels of education and literacy are directly connected to the personal hygiene. In short, people in undeveloped and low-income countries are more likely to be affected by all sorts of communicable diseases.

It is estimated that between 1.4 and 4.3 million people across the world are affected by cholera of whom 143,000 die every year. The Ebola outbreak in West Africa claimed more than 11,000 lives in 2014. Likewise, 36 million people worldwide are living with HIV/AIDS mainly in Sub-Saharan Africa [3]. What is more, we are witnessing the emergence of new communicable diseases every year. For example, more than 300 new communicable diseases have appeared between 1940 and 2004. It seems that genetic mutations and human-caused changes in the environment are responsible for the arrival of new viruses and bacteria. Among the recently emerged communicable outbreaks, SARS (Severe Acute Respiratory Syndrome) in 2003, the bird flu in 2006 through 2010, H1N1 influenza in 2009, Ebola in 2014, and MERS in 2015 have caused much harm and fear across the world and have received a good deal of coverage in the media.

The pandemics have always posed a serious threat to human beings, but for multiple reasons, the magnitude of their threat is becoming even more substantial in the recent decades. Industrialization, a massive urbanization across the world, a high density of livestock including pigs, poultry, and dairy cows, and the degradation of our natural environment have prepared a high-risk setting for the generation and transmission of communicable diseases. Furthermore, population growth, poverty, a lack of access to adequate sanitation, and lower health standards in many poor countries have provided an opportunity for a rapid transmission of pathogens. Above all, globalization and the increasing interconnectedness of the world's populations through travel, trade, and transport have facilitated the prompt spread of the new diseases across the planet. In the past decades, the volume of international travel has increased substantially and, as a result, people and products are moving faster across borders. As happened during the 2003 SARS epidemic, the high volume of international travel can play an important role in spreading the communicable diseases across the world. Therefore, the risks and impacts of epidemics are continuously growing over time. Based on a mathematical modeling, a serious communicable epidemic could spread to all major world cities within 60 days and kill more than 33 million people [3]. It is evident that a virulent outbreak, in addition to its direct mortality, will have serious socioeconomic implications. The recent experiences show, in order to fight or contain an epidemic, the governments customarily take measures to restrict regular activities and events, close schools and markets, and curb travels. In addition to the official measures, the panic of the disease may lead populations to limit or cancel their ordinary business activities and avoid public places. The fear of disease may have significant economic impacts even on the unaffected populations and countries. For instance, in the case of the SARS outbreak in 2003, some unaffected countries in East Asia experienced a 15 to 35 percent reduction in travel and tourism. According to the World Bank estimates, a virulent flu pandemic could cause $3 trillion in global economic losses, hence shrinking the world economic output by 4.8 percent [3]. Unemployment, market collapse, economic recession, social and political turmoil, poverty, and food insecurity are other consequences of an outbreak. According to the World Food Program, due to the Ebola outbreak in 2014, almost 200,000 people have become food insecure. A morbid epidemic not only could claim the lives of affected people, but also could paralyze the normal activities and functions of different societies, causing more death and damage, and thus creating a downward spiral in all spheres. Under these circumstances, the low-income countries that have insufficient resources will suffer the most.

The Rising Cost of Care and Shortage of Health Care Workers

Over the course of the next decades, higher levels of life expectancy and aging populations are supposed to put mounting pressure on health care networks in many developed and developing countries. As a result, the patients and governments have to spend much more in order to maintain the health care services at a decent level. In near future, the total global spending on health care is expected to increase by an annual average of 5.3 percent [8]. Since most of the societies are rapidly aging and the share of the economically active population is gradually shrinking, the higher expenditure on health care becomes a difficult proposition. For example, the working age population (15 to 64 years) in the European Union will decline by 48 million by 2050 [10]. In addition to aging and the shrinking portion of economically active populations, the overuse of medical services, overprescription of medications, and advances in treatments and health technologies will contribute to the rising cost of health care services across the world. As new treatments and technologies are developed, the drug makers hike the prices and send to their patient's bills heavier than ever. Some pharmaceutical companies have increased the drug prices as much as 5,000 to 6,000 percent in the past three years [18]. In 2015, Turing, an American drug maker, bought Daraprim, a 62-year-old medicine, for a deadly parasitic disease and then increased the price overnight from $13.50 to $750 a pill [19]. Those people who suffer from multiple chronic and long-term diseases will face more difficulty in getting the health care they need as their treatments are generally complex and expensive [11]. Regardless of their health care model, most countries across the world will experience unsustainable spending on their health care services [12]. In developed countries, the increasing share of older people will gradually place pressure on the health care spending. In such countries, acute care and institutional long-term care services are commonly available, but the aging populations increase the use of health care services and the per capita expenditures. By contrast, many developing countries simply do not have acute care and institutional long-term care services and are establishing baseline estimates of the prevalence and incidence of various diseases.

As well, the increasing pressure on the health care networks will result in a global shortage of health care workers. A study by the World Health Organization (WHO) revealed that, in 2013, out of 186 countries 118 suffered from a significant shortage of 7.2 million skilled health professionals [13]. Based on the same study, there will be a global shortage of almost 13 million health professionals in the next 20 years [13]. An additional 2 million health care workers across all European Union countries will be needed by 2020 [14]. While there is an increasing demand for health care services across the world, the health care workers are retiring or leaving for better-paid jobs without being replaced [13]. To overcome the shortages of their health care professionals, many high-income countries rely on foreign workers to meet their rising demands. In England around 35 percent and in Oman, the United Arab Emirates, and Saudi Arabia up to 80 percent of physicians are foreign nationals. Obviously, the migration of health professionals from low- to high-income countries creates an acute shortage in the home countries [15].

In the western developed countries, there have been major changes to the traditional nuclear family structure. In the past four decades, many western societies have seen the makeovers such as higher rates of divorce and remarriage, blended and step family relations, unmarried couples, single mothers, and same-sex relations. Because of these changes to the structure of nuclear families, older people will have few siblings and less familial care and support. The burden of these changes is supposed to grow over time. For example, in the United States the shares of divorced people for 65 and over, 55 to 64, and 45 to 54 are, respectively, 9, 17, and 18 percent [3]. This pattern implies that the level of family support to older people is expected to decline, as they will have increasingly fewer family relatives. The consequences of such changes to the family structure are more severe for women because unmarried women are less likely than unmarried men to accumulate assets and pension wealth for use in older age.

The Transformation of Social Insurance Systems

Currently, older people spend many years in retirement and are entitled to receive public funds for an extended period. Based on a study in OECD countries in 2007, the typical male worker could retire before age 64 and receive 18 years of retirement. Likewise, the average female worker could retire before age 63 and receive more than 22 years of pension's fund [2]. Increasing life expectancy and population aging result in the declining ratio of the workforce relative to the number of pensioners and necessarily strain the social insurance systems. An increasing number of countries across the world are reassessing the sustainability of their current social insurance systems. Facing a growing number of elderly people and retirees, many European countries have hiked taxes on workers' payrolls to collect more revenues. Other countries including Canada and the United States are encouraging tax incentives for individual retirement savings, contribution plans, and supplemental occupational pension [3]. Several countries including the United States, Japan, Iceland, and Norway have taken measures to transform their old-age social insurance programs by increasing the age at which workers become eligible to receive public pension benefits [3]. For instance, Japan increased the retirement age for men from 60 to 65 and for women from 57 to 65 in the past 10 years. Similarly, Norway and Iceland have raised the retirement age to 67 years. Since old-age dependency ratios are increasing in almost all countries of the world, the economic contributions of older people will gain more importance [1]. Therefore, the general trend is that many developed and developing countries want people to work for more years to compensate for the increasing costs of pensions and health care services. In addition to financial considerations, the senior workers possess valuable knowledge and job skills and show intact learning and thinking capacities that could benefit their employers [2]. Besides, there is some evidence that staying in the labor force after age 55 could have positive impacts on the mental and physical health of workers. Many older people can spend more years in the labor market if the jobs are accessible to them. Currently, most of the jobs even in the manufacturing sector require more cognitive skills and less physical effort. Therefore, continuing education, workplace rearrangement, and part-time employment opportunities for older workers will gain more importance.

References

[1] World Health Organization. 2003. *Global Health: Today's Challenges*. The World health report.

[2] World Health Organization. 2011. *Global Health and Aging*. Geneva: World Health Organization.

[3] Dobriansky, P.J., R.M. Suzman, and R.J. Hodes. 2007. "Why Population Aging Matters: A Global Perspective." National Institute on Aging, National Institutes of Health, US Department of Health and Human Services, US Department of State.

[4] Jonas, O.B. 2014. "Global Health Threats of the 21st Century." *Finance & Development* 51, no. 4.

[5] US Preventive Services Task Force. Screening and Behavioral Counseling Interventions in Primary Care to Reduce Alcohol Misuse: Recommendation Statement. US Preventive Services Task Force Website. http://uspreventiveservicestaskforce.org/3rduspstf/alcohol/alcomisrs.htm

[6] Task Force on Community Prevention Services. Preventing excessive alcohol consumption. The Guide to Community Preventive Services Website. http://thecommunityguide.org/alcohol/index.html

[7] Bloom, D., and R. McKinnon. 2010. "Introduction: Social Security and the Challenge of Demographic Change." *Program on the Global Demography of Aging*.

[8] World Healthcare Outlook, Economist Intelligence Unit, August 14, 2013.

[9] WHO 2011. Global Health and Ageing, National Institute on Ageing and National Institute of Health, U.S. Department of Health and Human Services.

[10] Commission of the European Communities 2008. Regions 2020. Demographic Challenges for European Regions [online], available at http://ec.europa.eu/regional_policy/sources/docoffic/working/regions2020/pdf/regions2020_demographic.pdf

[11] Deloitte 2015. 2015 Global Healthcare Outlook. Common Goals, Competing Priorities [online], available at https://deloitte.com/content/dam/Deloitte/global/Documents/Life-Sciences-Health-Care/gx-lshc-2015-health-care-outlook-global.pdf

[12] ACCA 2015. Sustainable Healthcare Systems: An International Study [online], available at https://leaders.accaglobal.com/content/dam/acca/global/PDF-technical/public-sector/tech-tp-sustainable-healthcaresystems.pdf

[13] Global Health Workforce Alliance and WHO 2013. A Universal Truth: No health without a workforce [online], available at http://who.int/workforcealliance/knowledge/resources/GHWA-a_universal_truth_report.pdf

[14] European Commission 2012. On an Action Plan for the EU Health Workforce [online], available at http://ec.europa.eu/dgs/health_consumer/docs/swd_ap_eu_healthcare_workforce_en.pdf

[15] Scrutton, J., G. Holley-Moore, and S.M. Bamford. Creating a Sustainable 21st Century Healthcare System.

[16] Billions have no access to toilets, says World Health Organisation report. https://theguardian.com/society/2015/jul/01/billions-have-no-access-to-toilets-says-world-health-organisation-report

[17] Eliminate Open Defecation | UNICEF, available at http://unicef.in/Whatwedo/11/Eliminate-Open-Defecation

[18] Forbes. February 10. 2017. "Why Did That Drug Price Increase 6,000%? It's The Lawhttps."//forbes.com/sites/matthewherper/2017/02/10/a-6000-price-hike-should-give-drug-companies-a-disgusting-sense-of-deja-vu/#7484c92771f5

[19] Los Angeles Times. December 21, 2016. "How 4 Drug Companies Rapidly Raised Prices on Life-Saving Drugs." http://latimes.com/business/la-fi-senate-drug-price-study-20161221-story.html

About the Author

Dr K.H. Yeganeh is a professor of international management at Winona State University in Minnesota. He has earned his MBA, MSc, and PhD from Université Laval in Quebec, Canada. His research focuses on global business and cross-cultural management. His scholarly research has appeared in various scholarly journals such as Journal of International Management, International Journal of Human Resource Management, International Journal of Cross-Cultural Management, Competitiveness Review, International Journal of Conflict Management, Cross-Cultural Management, and The Journal of East–West Business.

Index

OTHER TITLES IN THE INTERNATIONAL BUSINESS COLLECTION

Tamer Cavusgil, Georgia State; Michael Czinkota, Georgetown; and Gary Knight, Willamette University, Editors

- *As I See It...Views on International Business Crises, Innovations, and Freedom: The Impact on Our Daily Lives* by Michael R. Czinkota
- *A Strategic and Tactical Approach to Global Business Ethics, Second Edition* by Lawrence A. Beer
- *Innovation in China: The Tail of the Dragon* by William H.A. Johnson
- *Dancing With The Dragon: Doing Business With China* by Mona Chung and Bruno Mascitelli
- *Making Sense of Iranian Society, Culture, and Business* by Hamid Yeganeh
- *Tracing the Roots of Globalization and Business Principles, Second Edition* by Lawrence A. Beer
- *Creative Solutions to Global Business Negotiations, Second Edition* by Claude Cellich and Jain Subhash
- *Doing Business in Russia: A Concise Guide, Volume I* by Anatoly Zhuplev
- *Doing Business in Russia: A Concise Guide, Volume II* by Anatoly Zhuplev

Announcing the Business Expert Press Digital Library

Concise e-books business students need for classroom and research

This book can also be purchased in an e-book collection by your library as

- a one-time purchase,
- that is owned forever,
- allows for simultaneous readers,
- has no restrictions on printing, and
- can be downloaded as PDFs from within the library community.

Our digital library collections are a great solution to beat the rising cost of textbooks. E-books can be loaded into their course management systems or onto student's e-book readers.
The **Business Expert Press** digital libraries are very affordable, with no obligation to buy in future years. For more information, please visit **www.businessexpertpress.com/librarians**. To set up a trial in the United States, please email **sales@businessexpertpress.com**.

www.ingramcontent.com/pod-product-compliance
Lightning Source LLC
Chambersburg PA
CBHW060538210326
41519CB00014B/3256